NEXTEXT TEACHER'S RESOURCE MANUAL

REFORMATION AND ENLIGHTENMENT

1500–1800

nextext

Printed in the United States of America

ISBN 0-618-15411-6

2 3 4 5 6 7 — PBO — 06 05 04 03

Table of Contents

Selections and Quizzes

Each selection has a full lesson plan that includes:

- **Background**
- **People and Terms to Know**
- **After Reading Questions**
- **Bibliography**
- **Study Guide**
- **Vocabulary Quiz**
- **Answer Key**

PART 1: RELIGION AND RELIGIOUS WARS

Stories in History

Stories in History is a series of easy-reading books that provide stories about the interesting people and pivotal events of history in the lively, narrative style of good fiction. Each title in the series takes a different historical period that matches the curriculum. Maps and time lines are included where needed to aid student understanding. The 13 to 16 stories in a book are enlivened by drawings, paintings, cartoons, documents, photos, and other artifacts. Thus, the authenticity of the real-life people and events is underscored. Suggestions for students' further reading are provided.

Books in the Series

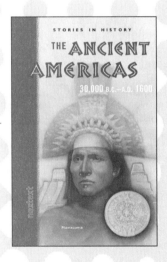

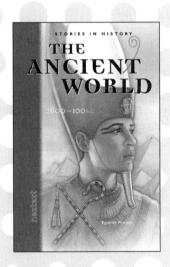

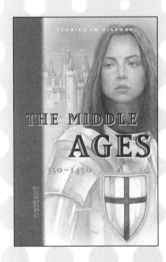

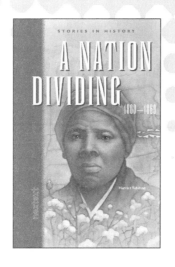

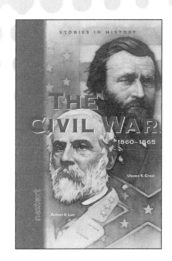

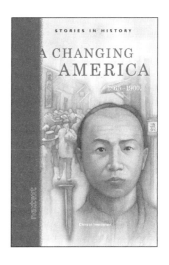

Overview

The Reformation and Enlightenment contains many tales that give insight into the remarkable changes in human thought and behavior that occurred between 1500 and 1800. These changes occurred in the relationship between religion and the state, in the way people approached the study of nature and their own minds and bodies, and in the wealth of new ideas that arose during this "Age of Reason."

Many of the changes of this time are best understood through the lives of the people who literally changed history. Stories about Martin Luther and Ignatius Loyola show us the causes and direction of religious reform. Cardinal Richelieu, Catherine the Great, Marie Antoinette, and Thomas Jefferson demonstrate the range of human abilities and achievements.

Readers are also invited to explore the effects of exploration and conquest on both the Old and New World, to experience the great slave revolt in Haiti, and to suffer through the fears of smallpox with an English mother of the early 1700s. *The Reformation and Enlightenment* strives to present a balanced yet intriguing look at this remarkable period of history that laid the groundwork for modern society.

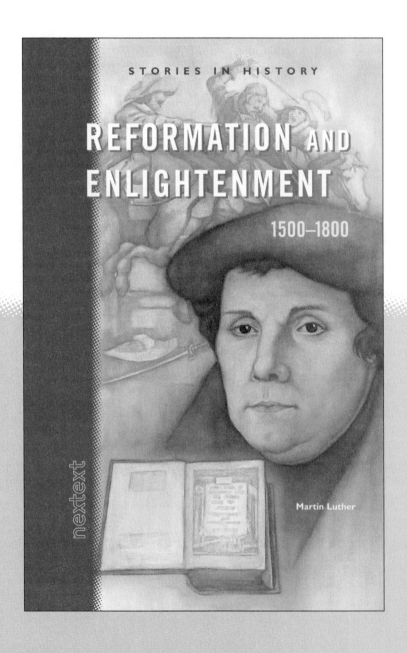

STORIES IN HISTORY

REFORMATION AND ENLIGHTENMENT

1500–1800

nextext

Martin Luther

Using *The Reformation and Enlightenment TRM*

Organization of the Teacher's Resource Manual

Each lesson in this manual is divided into four short sections that give instructors valuable background and assessment tools.

❶ Before Reading

Background

For each of the main selections in the reader, extensive background has been provided to help teachers prepare and extend their teaching. The background sections help to set the context for the selection and explain the circumstances surrounding the historical time and people involved.

People and Terms to Know

All of the vocabulary words highlighted in the selection in the student's reader have been included here in the **Teacher's Resource Manual**. Inclusion of these vocabulary words allows teachers to expand on the **Building Vocabulary** exercise included later in the lesson and gives vocabulary more emphasis.

Text Pages 28–39

The Trial of Martin Luther

BY LYNNETTE BRENT

Before Reading

Background

"The Trial of Martin Luther" takes place in 1521. Luther is often credited with instigating the period known as the Reformation. In truth, many different factors converged at this point in history, allowing Luther's ideas to fall on fertile ground.

Modern historians find it difficult to assess the exact reasons for the Reformation. Catholic writings of the time insist that much reform was already going on before the time of Luther and the rise of Protestantism. Protestant writings painted the late medieval Church in the worst possible terms to prove the necessity of a complete break with such a corrupt past.

Pious Catholics in Spain, Italy, Germany, France, and England were already disgusted with abuses by the papacy, the clergy, and some religious monks and nuns. Several popes led degenerate lives. In the late 1400s, for example, Innocent VIII performed marriage ceremonies for his own illegitimate children. Many high clergy led lives of wealth and ease while demanding more money from the poor to support luxurious projects.

Several well-known churchmen had already spoken up for reform. William of Ockham had gone so far as to say that when the Church was in danger of heresy, it was up to laypeople to see to its reform.

At the same time, as Europe emerged from the late Middle Ages, nationalist spirit was growing. There had long been an intimate relationship between the papacy and the Holy Roman Emperors. As countries began to assert their independence and monarchs acquired new power, they felt the need to assert themselves against the papacy and local church rule.

It was against this background that Lu[ther] his tortured efforts to return the Church t[o] he saw as its original purpose—the spirit[ual] development of its members. As a well-e[ducated] Augustinian monk, Luther believed in str[ict] discipline among the clergy. He was appa[lled by] worldliness and wealthy lifestyles of the [clergy in] Rome. Luther felt that he must speak out [against] these practices and the rising abuse of ind[ulgences.]

Originally, the doctrine of indulgences [held that] although sin was forgiven through the sac[rament of] penance, justice demanded that some pun[ishment] must be exacted for the "crime." These pu[nishments] could take the form of fasting, prayer, giv[ing to] the poor, or contributions for religious pu[rposes. The] belief was that some people did so much [that] their sins that they built up a surplus. The C[hurch] then permitted to distribute this surplus [to] people through indulgences.

Over time, people began to believe tha[t they] could buy their way out of purgatory. Th[ey could] even pay for future sins and "bail" decea[sed friends] and relatives out of purgatory. Abuse of t[he] indulgences had grown rampant in Luthe[r's time.] His 95 theses were not a declaration of wa[r on] the church, but an honest call for discussi[on of] these abuses and the need for reform.

Preteaching the Story

Direct students to read the Background p[aragraphs on] "The Reformation" and "The Rise of Prot[estantism."] Use the story title as a starting point for s[peculation.] What do they expect the story to be abou[t? What do] they think they may learn from reading t[he story?] Record students' predictions and expecta[tions.]

2 Stories of the Reformation and Enlightenment TRM

Students may find the "Diet of Worms" amusing. Explain that this sort of "Diet" is an assembly of important people. Mention that Japan's lawmaking body is still referred to as a diet. "Worms" is a town in Germany. It has the German pronunciation of "vahrmz."

Fact or Fiction?

The narrator and his family are fictional characters. The events described in the story are historically accurate. Luther's reason for becoming a monk has been questioned and is considered a legend. It is also now believed that he never actually nailed the 95 theses to the cathedral door. He did send them to his church superiors, asking for discussion and clarification. Nailing them to the door of the church would have been seen as a direct insult to his superiors. This is something that Luther was unlikely to have done at that point in his life.

Students will find sources for this story at the back of their book, on page 181.

Tie-in to History and Geography

When Pope Leo III crowned Charlemagne "Emperor of the Romans" in A.D. 800, the title had little to do with Rome. Leo was acknowledging Charlemagne's efforts to unite Europe as the old Roman Empire had once done. However, it established a unique relationship between Germany and Italy that continued for more than 800 years. For a time, the "Holy Roman Emperor" decided who would be pope and claimed the right to appoint bishops. Later, the papacy began to use the threat of excommunication to control politics in Germany and other European countries, such as England.

The struggle for power between the Holy Roman Empire and the papacy had already led a number of church scholars in various countries to call for reforms before Luther's 95 theses. By that time, the Holy Roman Empire had grown to include Belgium, the Netherlands, Austria, Spain, and the Spanish lands in the Americas.

People and Terms to Know

Martin Luther—(1483–1546) German-born leader of the Protestant Reformation. He wrote books about religion, translated the Bible, wrote a system for education, and wrote songs still sung in churches today.

heretic—person accused of heresy, of believing things that go against the teachings of the Catholic Church.

monastery (MAHN•uh•STEHR•ee)—community or building where monks live.

Diet of Worms—(1521) famous government meeting called by the Holy Roman Emperor Charles V to decide what to do about the problem of Protestantism. It was held in Worms, Germany, where Martin Luther was found guilty of heresy.

Charles V—(1500–1558) king of Spain and emperor of the Holy Roman Empire 1519–1556. His empire included Belgium, the Netherlands, Austria, Spain, and the Spanish lands in the Americas. He belonged to the powerful Hapsburg family.

indulgences—in the Roman Catholic Church, special favors to avoid punishment for sins, both on earth and after death. The Church forbade the sale of indulgences in 1562 at the Council of Trent.

95 theses—famous statement of beliefs published by Martin Luther.

excommunicated—formally expelled from membership in the Church.

Reformation—the word means "restructuring or change." In the 1500s, the Protestant Reformation rejected or changed some of the teachings of the Roman Catholic Church. This resulted in the formation of new churches.

Protestant—referring to one of the Christian churches that resulted from the Reformation, such as Lutheran, Baptist, and so on.

John Calvin—(1509–1564) French Protestant founder of Calvinism. He studied religion and law in France and tried to start a government that was based on religious law.

Ulrich Zwingli (ZWIHNG•lee)—(1484–1531) Roman Catholic priest in Switzerland who believed in Martin Luther's ideas. He founded the Reformed Church.

(Tested vocabulary words used in the online vocabulary quiz are underlined.)

The Trial of Martin Luther 3

❷ During Reading

At this point, students are directed to read the selection itself and use the **Study Guide** included later in this lesson.

During Reading

Have your students use the **Study Guide** on the next page to help them understand and enjoy the story and recognize its importance in history.

After Reading

Have your students answer the **Questions to Consider** in the book as a way to deepen their interpretation of the selection.

1. How did Martin Luther's visit to Rome change his thinking?

2. Why did Luther oppose the sale of indulgences?

3. How did Martin Luther share his ideas? What was the result?

4. Why do you think that Charles V handed down such a harsh punishment for Luther?

5. What do you think would have happened to the Reformation if Charles V's sentence had been carried out?

Bibliography

Martin Luther

Edwin P. Booth and Dan Harmon. *Martin Luther: The Great Reformer* (1998). Recognizing from Romans 1 that God gives believers in Christ a positive righteousness, Luther refused to be silenced and became a great reformer.

Judith O'Neill. *Martin Luther* (1979). Presents the life and philosophy of a key figure in the Protestant Reformation.

Julia Pferdehirt, Dave Jackson, Neta Jackson. *Spy for the Night Riders: Martin Luther* (2000). After coming to Wittenberg to seek an education, Karl Schumacher becomes a student of Dr. Martin Luther and, when the latter is declared a heretic, Karl accompanies him when he travels to Worms to defend his views. (Fiction.)

Sally Stepanek. *Martin Luther* (1986). A biography of the German monk who led the Protestant Reformation in Europe from its beginning in 1517 until his death in 1546.

Bill Yenne. *100 Men Who Shaped World History* (1994). Includes a biography of the life of Martin Luther.

The Reformation

Sarah Flowers. *The Reformation* (1995). Historical overview of the Protestant Reformation from its initial stirrings in medieval times through the Counter Reformation, and its cultural effects.

Michael Mullett. *The Reformation* (1996). History of the Reformation and the Counter Reformation in the sixteenth century.

Robert G. Shearer. *Famous Men of the Renaissance and Reformation* (1996). Includes the leaders of the Protestant movement during the Reformation.

Sally Stepanek. *John Calvin* (1987). Biography of the French Protestant leader who started Calvinism.

Stephen P. Thompson. *The Reformation* (1999). A history of the Reformation in the sixteenth century.

❸ After Reading

Questions to Consider

Each of the **Questions to Consider** at the end of the selection in the student's reader is given here for teachers to use and review as they prepare to teach the selection. Answers to these questions are given after the **Vocabulary Quiz** in the **Teacher's Resource Manual.**

Bibliography

The selection is then followed by an extensive **Bibliography** of other sources and materials that teachers may consult. The **Bibliography** includes a comprehensive list of authoritative sources for teachers to consult in preparing to teach the selection.

During Reading

Have your students use the **Study Guide** on the next page to help them understand and enjoy the story and recognize its importance in history.

After Reading

Have your students answer the **Questions to Consider** in the book as a way to deepen their interpretation of the selection.

1. How did Martin Luther's visit to Rome change his thinking?

2. Why did Luther oppose the sale of indulgences?

3. How did Martin Luther share his ideas? What was the result?

4. Why do you think that Charles V handed down such a harsh punishment for Luther?

5. What do you think would have happened to the Reformation if Charles V's sentence had been carried out?

Bibliography

Martin Luther

Edwin P. Booth and Dan Harmon. *Martin Luther: The Great Reformer* (1998). Recognizing from Romans 1 that God gives believers in Christ a positive righteousness, Luther refused to be silenced and became a great reformer.

Judith O'Neill. *Martin Luther* (1979). Presents the life and philosophy of a key figure in the Protestant Reformation.

Julia Pferdehirt, Dave Jackson, Neta Jackson. *Spy for the Night Riders: Martin Luther* (2000). After coming to Wittenberg to seek an education, Karl Schumacher becomes a student of Dr. Martin Luther and, when the latter is declared a heretic, Karl accompanies him when he travels to Worms to defend his views. (Fiction.)

Sally Stepanek. *Martin Luther* (1986). A biography of the German monk who led the Protestant Reformation in Europe from its beginning in 1517 until his death in 1546.

Bill Yenne. *100 Men Who Shaped World History* (1994). Includes a biography of the life of Martin Luther.

The Reformation

Sarah Flowers. *The Reformation* (1995). Historical overview of the Protestant Reformation from its initial stirrings in medieval times through the Counter Reformation, and its cultural effects.

Michael Mullett. *The Reformation* (1996). History of the Reformation and the Counter Reformation in the sixteenth century.

Robert G. Shearer. *Famous Men of the Renaissance and Reformation* (1996). Includes the leaders of the Protestant movement during the Reformation.

Sally Stepanek. *John Calvin* (1987). Biography of the French Protestant leader who started Calvinism.

Stephen P. Thompson. *The Reformation* (1999). A history of the Reformation in the sixteenth century.

4   **Stories of the Reformation and Enlightenment TRM**

Study Guide

In order to help student's comprehension of the selection, the **Study Guide** walks students through the reading, asking the pertinent questions that will help build understanding. Answers to the questions in the **Study Guide** are given in the **Answer Key** at the end of this lesson.

Vocabulary Quiz

The purpose of the **Vocabulary Quiz** is to build students' recognition and acquisition of new words. Many of the selections in the reader introduce new terms appropriate to a specific period (for example, Iron Curtain). Other selections include academic vocabulary that may be unfamiliar to some students or that may be useful for them to acquire as they prepare for taking standardized tests. The **Vocabulary Quiz** selects 5 key words and gives teachers a fast, convenient way to encourage students learning new words.

Study Guide

Name _____

The Trial of Martin Luther
by Lynnette Brent

1. What caused Martin Luther to give up studying law to become a r

_____

_____

_____

2. How did Luther believe that a person could be forgiven for doing

_____

_____

_____

3. In his 95 theses, what reason did Luther give for the pope and the

_____

_____

_____

4. What did Charles V insist that Martin Luther do to avoid being th

_____

_____

_____

5. Essay Question
Why do you think that Charles may have waited until after Marti
before issuing the Edict that called Luther an outlaw?

Building Vocabulary

Name _____

People and Terms to Know

This page lets you check your knowledge of the people and the terms used in "The Trial of Martin Luther." Find the best answer for each item. Then circle that answer.

1. This was a movement in which some people rejected or changed some of the teachings of the Catholic Church.

   a. Martin Luther
   b. Charles V
   c. Diet of Worms
   d. Reformation

2. Which person wrote a list of statements about the way the Church handled indulgences?

   a. Martin Luther
   b. Charles V
   c. Kurt
   d. Ulrich Zwingli

3. Which is the best description of a Protestant?

   a. person who protests religious ideas
   b. person who believed in the ideas of Martin Luther
   c. type of Christian church that arose during the Reformation
   d. decree that formally expels a person from church membership

4. This term describes a meeting or assembly of leaders in a German city.

   a. Treaty of Versailles
   b. Council of Trent
   c. Diet of Worms
   d. Reformation

5. Which person was an emperor of the Holy Roman Empire?

   a. Martin Luther
   b. Charles V
   c. John Calvin
   d. Johann Eck

❹ Answers

The **Answer Key** gives teachers examples of how students may respond to the questions posed in the "After Reading," "Study Guide," "Essay Question," and "Building Vocabulary" sections. Teachers can use these answers as guides for assessing students, or they can provide the answers to the class as a study aid.

Answer Key

The Trial of Martin Luther
by Lynnette Brent

After Reading

1. Martin Luther was troubled about the way priests were living and the way that they sold indulgences.
2. Luther said that priests couldn't guarantee that a person would be saved. He said that people got the impression that they didn't have to be sorry for what they had done to be forgiven. All they had to do was buy enough indulgences.
3. He wrote his ideas in the 95 theses and nailed them to the door of the church so that people could read them. This got him in trouble with the Catholic Church and with the Holy Roman Emperor Charles V. He was brought to trial in Worms in 1521.
4. Answers will vary. Some students may say that he didn't like that Luther would criticize the Church. Others may suggest that he couldn't let someone question Church teachings, that the Church pressured him, or that he was somehow gaining from the sale of indulgences.
5. Answers will vary. Some students may say that the Reformation would not have gone forward and that Protestant religions wouldn't have been formed. Others may say that the people would have rebelled and the Reformation still would have occurred.

Study Guide

Answers will vary. Possible answers follow.
1. According to legend, he was knocked to the ground by lightning and promised St. Anne that he would become a monk if she rescued him.
2. He believed that forgiveness could come if a person was truly sorry for doing wrong. People should also have faith that God would forgive them.
3. He said that the pope and the Church were selling indulgences to get money and that they didn't care about people's salvation.
4. He wanted Luther to take back everything he had said and admit he was wrong.

5. Essay Question Some students may suggest that Charles V wanted someone else to do the dirty work of getting rid of Martin Luther. That way, he couldn't be accused of killing him. Others may say that Martin Luther had many friends who agreed with him. They would have made trouble if they had still been in Worms when Charles made his decree. Students should support their answers with reasons.

Building Vocabulary
Answers: 1. d, 2. a, 3. c, 4. c, 5. b.

Web Resources

The Nextext web site offers valuable teaching and learning support for all the Nextext products. Online background information, quizzes, links, and answer keys help teachers and students save time and money.

When you adopt a classroom set of a Nextext title, you gain access to these Nextext web site resources.

You are given teacher and student code numbers to access various pages. You can issue the student code to your entire classroom, giving students access to self-assessment tools and independent research and review, or you can use only the teacher code and print out the student resources as quizzes or homework assignments.

On the Nextext web site, you can find:

- **Additional background information**
- **Worksheets and study guides that can be printed out**
- **Self-scoring quizzes with immediate feedback**
- **Bibliographies to help with student research projects**
- **Lists of relevant links on the web for further study**
- **Answer keys for teachers**

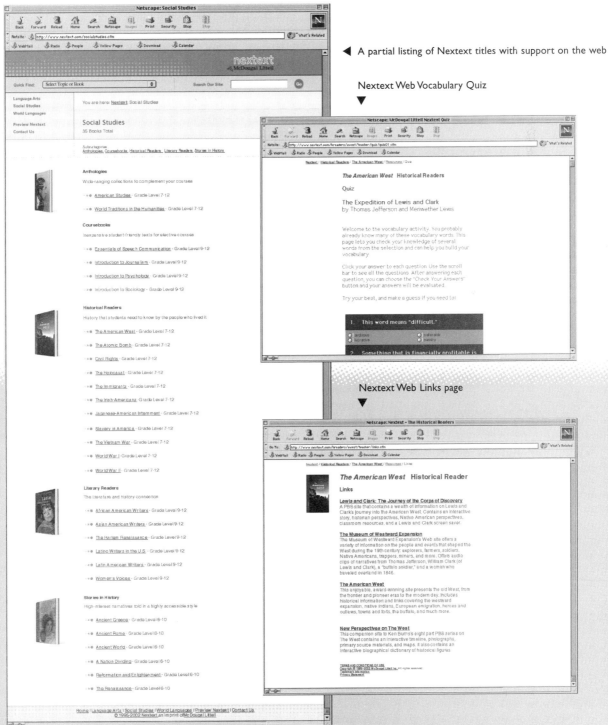

◀ A partial listing of Nextext titles with support on the web

Nextext Web Vocabulary Quiz
▼

Nextext Web Links page
▼

Web Links for *The Reformation and Enlightenment*

Martin Luther

http://www.luther.de/e/worms.html

Students can click on links to find out more about indulgences, Luther's appearance before the Diet of Worms, and the repurcussions of his nailing the 95 Theses to the door of the Wittenberg cathedral. This very deep site includes excellent pictures of various aspects of Luther's life. There is a section on legends, such as his reason for becoming a monk rather than a lawyer.

The Shaping of Modern Europe

http://www.saburchill.com/history/chapters/chapters.html

Part of The Open Door website written in France for students aged 9-17, this page contains links to many of the topics in the age of Reformation and the Enlightenment. Items are brief but informative and include relevant pictures.

The Enlightenment

http://www.mrdowling.com/705french.html

This teacher-produced site contains a one-page explanation of the Enlightenment, connecting it to Galileo and the French and American revolutions. It contains a map.

Thomas Jefferson and Monticello

http://www.monticello.org/

Links allow students to follow Jefferson through a typical day, tour his house and plantation, and get a real sense of what life was like in his time. The website has quotes and pictures as well as information about daily life in America during the late eighteenth and early nineteenth century.

The French Revolution

http://www.mrdowling.com/705-frenchrevolution.html

This site is also referenced for The Enlightenment. The page contains an explanation of the French Revolution that includes information about Louis XVI and a picture of him. Also included is information about Marie Antoinette, the guillotine, and the storming of the Bastille.

The Columbian Exchange

http://daphne.palomar.edu/scrout/colexc.htm

After students read a brief explanation of the Columbian Exchange, they can click on links that explain how various foods, diseases, and horses influenced the culture of the Old and New Worlds. Other links explain how the exchange influenced ideas about liberty, business, and ecology.

Exploring Amistad

http://amistad.mysticseaport.org

This site provides information about the Slave Revolt aboard the Amistad, a ship carrying slaves in the 1800s. The site relates to both the Columbian Exchange and the story on Touissant L'Overture. Included are many links to related information such as a page on the Middle Passage.

The Galileo Project

http://es.rice.edu/ES/humsoc/Galileo/index.html

The recipient of a number of educational awards, this site gives students the opportunity to learn more about Galileo's life and accomplishments. There are timelines, maps, pictures of his villa, and links to various projects that he undertook in his life. People, places, and things that were important in Galileo's life are described and explained. The site contains many pictures.

The Trial of Martin Luther

BY LYNNETTE BRENT

Before Reading

Background

"The Trial of Martin Luther" takes place in 1521. Luther is often credited with instigating the period known as the Reformation. In truth, many different factors converged at this point in history, allowing Luther's ideas to fall on fertile ground.

Modern historians find it difficult to assess the exact reasons for the Reformation. Catholic writings of the time insist that much reform was already going on before the time of Luther and the rise of Protestantism. Protestant writings painted the late medieval Church in the worst possible terms to prove the necessity of a complete break with such a corrupt past.

Pious Catholics in Spain, Italy, Germany, France, and England were already disgusted with abuses by the papacy, the clergy, and some religious monks and nuns. Several popes led degenerate lives. In the late 1400s, for example, Innocent VIII performed marriage ceremonies for his own illegitimate children. Many high clergy led lives of wealth and ease while demanding more money from the poor to support luxurious projects.

Several well-known churchmen had already spoken up for reform. William of Ockham had gone so far as to say that when the Church was in danger of heresy, it was up to laypeople to see to its reform.

At the same time, as Europe emerged from the late Middle Ages, nationalist spirit was growing. There had long been an intimate relationship between the papacy and the Holy Roman Emperors. As countries began to assert their independence and monarchs acquired new power, they felt the need to assert themselves against the papacy and local church rule.

It was against this background that Luther began his tortured efforts to return the Church to what he saw as its original purpose—the spiritual development of its members. As a well-educated Augustinian monk, Luther believed in strong discipline among the clergy. He was appalled at the worldliness and wealthy lifestyles of the clergy in Rome. Luther felt that he must speak out against these practices and the rising abuse of indulgences.

Originally, the doctrine of indulgences stated that, although sin was forgiven through the sacrament of penance, justice demanded that some punishment must be exacted for the "crime." These punishments could take the form of fasting, prayer, giving alms to the poor, or contributions for religious purposes. The belief was that some people did so much penance for their sins that they built up a surplus. The Church was then permitted to distribute this surplus to worthy people through indulgences.

Over time, people began to believe that they could buy their way out of purgatory. They could even pay for future sins and "bail" deceased friends and relatives out of purgatory. Abuse of the sale of indulgences had grown rampant in Luther's time. His 95 theses were not a declaration of war against the church, but an honest call for discussion about these abuses and the need for reform.

Preteaching the Story

Direct students to read the Background pages 11–12, "The Reformation" and "The Rise of Protestantism." Use the story title as a starting point for students. What do they expect the story to be about? What do they think they may learn from reading this story? Record students' predictions and expectations.

Students may find the "Diet of Worms" amusing. Explain that this sort of "Diet" is an assembly of important people. Mention that Japan's lawmaking body is still referred to as a diet. "Worms" is a town in Germany. It has the German pronunciation of "vahrmz."

Fact or Fiction?

The narrator and his family are fictional characters. The events described in the story are historically accurate. Luther's reason for becoming a monk has been questioned and is considered a legend. It is also now believed that he never actually nailed the 95 theses to the cathedral door. He did send them to his church superiors, asking for discussion and clarification. Nailing them to the door of the church would have been seen as a direct insult to his superiors. This is something that Luther was unlikely to have done at that point in his life.

Students will find sources for this story at the back of their book, on page 181.

Tie-in to History and Geography

When Pope Leo III crowned Charlemagne "Emperor of the Romans" in A.D. 800, the title had little to do with Rome. Leo was acknowledging Charlemagne's efforts to unite Europe as the old Roman Empire had once done. However, it established a unique relationship between Germany and Italy that continued for more than 800 years. For a time, the "Holy Roman Emperor" decided who would be pope and claimed the right to appoint bishops. Later, the papacy began to use the threat of excommunication to control politics in Germany and other European countries, such as England.

The struggle for power between the Holy Roman Empire and the papacy had already led a number of church scholars in various countries to call for reforms before Luther's 95 theses. By that time, the Holy Roman Empire had grown to include Belgium, the Netherlands, Austria, Spain, and the Spanish lands in the Americas.

People and Terms to Know

Martin Luther—(1483–1546) German-born leader of the Protestant Reformation. He wrote books about religion, translated the Bible, formed a system for education, and wrote songs still sung in churches today.

heretic—person accused of heresy, of believing things that go against the teachings of the Catholic Church.

monastery (MAHN•uh•STEHR•ee)—community or building where monks live.

Diet of Worms—(1521) famous government meeting called by the Holy Roman Emperor Charles V to decide what to do about the problem of Protestantism. It was held in Worms, Germany, where Martin Luther was found guilty of heresy.

Charles V—(1500–1558) king of Spain and emperor of the Holy Roman Empire 1519–1556. His empire included Belgium, the Netherlands, Austria, Spain, and the Spanish lands in the Americas. He belonged to the powerful Hapsburg family.

indulgences—in the Roman Catholic Church, special favors to avoid punishment for sins, both on earth and after death. The Church forbade the sale of indulgences in 1562 at the Council of Trent.

95 theses—famous statement of beliefs published by Martin Luther.

excommunicated—formally expelled from membership in the Church.

Reformation—the word means "restructuring or change." In the 1500s, the Protestant Reformation rejected or changed some of the teachings of the Roman Catholic Church. This resulted in the formation of new churches.

Protestant—referring to one of the Christian churches that resulted from the Reformation, such as Lutheran, Baptist, and so on.

John Calvin—(1509–1564) French Protestant founder of Calvinism. He studied religion and law in France and tried to start a government that was based on religious law.

Ulrich Zwingli (ZWIHNG•lee)—(1484–1531) Roman Catholic priest in Switzerland who believed in Martin Luther's ideas. He founded the Reformed Church.

(Tested vocabulary words used in the online vocabulary quiz are underlined.)

During Reading

Have your students use the **Study Guide** on the next page to help them understand and enjoy the story and recognize its importance in history.

After Reading

Have your students answer the **Questions to Consider** in the book as a way to deepen their interpretation of the selection.

1. How did Martin Luther's visit to Rome change his thinking?

2. Why did Luther oppose the sale of indulgences?

3. How did Martin Luther share his ideas? What was the result?

4. Why do you think that Charles V handed down such a harsh punishment for Luther?

5. What do you think would have happened to the Reformation if Charles V's sentence had been carried out?

Bibliography

Martin Luther

Edwin P. Booth and Dan Harmon. *Martin Luther: The Great Reformer* (1998). Recognizing from Romans 1 that God gives believers in Christ a positive righteousness, Luther refused to be silenced and became a great reformer.

Judith O'Neill. *Martin Luther* (1979). Presents the life and philosophy of a key figure in the Protestant Reformation.

Julia Pferdehirt, Dave Jackson, Neta Jackson. *Spy for the Night Riders: Martin Luther* (2000). After coming to Wittenberg to seek an education, Karl Schumacher becomes a student of Dr. Martin Luther and, when the latter is declared a heretic, Karl accompanies him when he travels to Worms to defend his views. (Fiction.)

Sally Stepanek. *Martin Luther* (1986). A biography of the German monk who led the Protestant Reformation in Europe from its beginning in 1517 until his death in 1546.

Bill Yenne. *100 Men Who Shaped World History* (1994). Includes a biography of the life of Martin Luther.

The Reformation

Sarah Flowers. *The Reformation* (1995). Historical overview of the Protestant Reformation from its initial stirrings in medieval times through the Counter Reformation, and its cultural effects.

Michael Mullett. *The Reformation* (1996). History of the Reformation and the Counter Reformation in the sixteenth century.

Robert G. Shearer. *Famous Men of the Renaissance and Reformation* (1996). Includes the leaders of the Protestant movement during the Reformation.

Sally Stepanek. *John Calvin* (1987). Biography of the French Protestant leader who started Calvinism.

Stephen P. Thompson. *The Reformation* (1999). A history of the Reformation in the sixteenth century.

Name _____

The Trial of Martin Luther
by Lynnette Brent

1. What caused Martin Luther to give up studying law to become a monk?

_____

_____

_____

2. How did Luther believe that a person could be forgiven for doing wrong?

_____

_____

_____

3. In his 95 theses, what reason did Luther give for the pope and the Church selling indulgences?

_____

_____

_____

4. What did Charles V insist that Martin Luther do to avoid being thrown into prison?

_____

_____

_____

5. Essay Question
   Why do you think that Charles may have waited until after Martin Luther had left the Diet of Worms before issuing the Edict that called Luther an outlaw?

Name

People and Terms to Know

This page lets you check your knowledge of the people and the terms used in "The Trial of Martin Luther." Find the best answer for each item. Then circle that answer.

1. This was a movement in which some people rejected or changed some of the teachings of the Catholic Church.

   a. Martin Luther

   b. Charles V

   c. Diet of Worms

   d. Reformation

2. Which person wrote a list of statements about the way the Church handled indulgences?

   a. Martin Luther

   b. Charles V

   c. Kurt

   d. Ulrich Zwingli

3. Which is the best description of a Protestant?

   a. person who protests religious ideas

   b. person who believed in the ideas of Martin Luther

   c. type of Christian church that arose during the Reformation

   d. decree that formally expels a person from church membership

4. This term describes a meeting or assembly of leaders in a German city.

   a. Treaty of Versailles

   b. Council of Trent

   c. Diet of Worms

   d. Reformation

5. Which person was an emperor of the Holy Roman Empire?

   a. Martin Luther

   b. Charles V

   c. John Calvin

   d. Johann Eck

The Trial of Martin Luther
by Lynnette Brent

After Reading

1. Martin Luther was troubled about the way priests were living and the way that they sold indulgences.
2. Luther said that priests couldn't guarantee that a person would be saved. He said that people got the impression that they didn't have to be sorry for what they had done to be forgiven. All they had to do was buy enough indulgences.
3. He wrote his ideas in the 95 theses and nailed them to the door of the church so that people could read them. This got him in trouble with the Catholic Church and with the Holy Roman Emperor Charles V. He was brought to trial in Worms in 1521.
4. Answers will vary. Some students may say that he didn't like that Luther would criticize the Church. Others may suggest that he couldn't let someone question Church teachings, that the Church pressured him, or that he was somehow gaining from the sale of indulgences.
5. Answers will vary. Some students may say that the Reformation would not have gone forward and that Protestant religions wouldn't have been formed. Others may say that the people would have rebelled and the Reformation still would have occurred.

Study Guide

Answers will vary. Possible answers follow.
1. According to legend, he was knocked to the ground by lightning and promised St. Anne that he would become a monk if she rescued him.
2. He believed that forgiveness could come if a person was truly sorry for doing wrong. People should also have faith that God would forgive them.
3. He said that the pope and the Church were selling indulgences to get money and that they didn't care about people's salvation.
4. He wanted Luther to take back everything he had said and admit he was wrong.

5. Essay Question Some students may suggest that Charles V wanted someone else to do the dirty work of getting rid of Martin Luther. That way, he couldn't be accused of killing him. Others may say that Martin Luther had many friends who agreed with him. They would have made trouble if they had still been in Worms when Charles made his decree. Students should support their answers with reasons.

Building Vocabulary

Answers: **1.** d, **2.** a, **3.** c, **4.** c, **5.** b.

Text Pages 40–48

From Soldier to Saint

BY WALTER HAZEN

Before Reading

Background

"From Soldier to Saint" is the story of Ignatius Loyola, one of the most influential figures in the Catholic Reformation of the 1500s. The Church was already suffering from a decline of its political power, a decline which had begun as early as the 1200s. At the end of the Middle Ages, with the rise of the middle class in western Europe, many of the Church's traditional practices, such as the ban on charging interest on loans, were seen as obstacles to financial growth.

By the end of the 1400s, the various Church councils had failed to bring about reform. Professional theologians seemed more interested in debating scholastic issues than nurturing Christian faith and life. The financial corruption and immorality in the highest ranks of the Church were reason enough for forces within the Church itself to take matters into their own hands.

In response to the Protestant Reformation, the Church undertook its own Reformation—the Catholic Reformation. The Council of Trent took place between 1545 and 1563. It led to many changes in the internal life and discipline of the Church. New religious orders were established, among them the Society of Jesus—or Jesuits— founded by Ignatius Loyola. Unlike the Benedictines, Dominicans, and Franciscans, the Jesuits dedicated themselves to reconstructing Church life and teaching in the wake of the Protestant Reformation.

As the story tells, Ignatius Loyola was born in 1491 and trained as a knight in the service of the Viceroy of Navarre. Although he stood under five feet two inches, he was, by his own admission, "a man given to the vanities of the world, whose chief delight consisted in martial exercises, with a great and vain desire to win renown."

The lives of the saints that he read during his convalescence described the service of God as holy chivalry. This appealed to Loyola and he vowed to live a more austere life in payment for his previous sins. He first traveled to Montserrat where he spent three days confessing the sins of his whole life and then hung his sword and dagger near the statue of the Virgin Mary to symbolize his abandonment of his previous ambition. From there, he traveled to Manresa, where he began his spiritual practice.

Convinced of the importance of good preparation, perhaps by his military career, Loyola put off becoming a priest for 12 years. During that time, he studied and spent time in the classroom, years after most men his age would have bothered.

By 1526, in his mid-30s, Loyola had already begun preaching and had attracted several followers. He was imprisoned several times and finally decided to stay out of the public eye until he became a priest. In the 1530s, while studying in Paris, he gathered the band that would join him in founding the Society of Jesus. They took vows of poverty, chastity, and obedience, although they were not yet a religious order. It was not until 1537 that Loyola and most of his followers were ordained to the priesthood. In 1540, Pope Paul III approved the plan for the Jesuits and the order officially formed.

Preteaching the Story

To help students with background information, direct them to pages 12–13, "Catholic Reformation."

Use the story title as a starting point for students. What do they expect the story to be about? What does the picture and caption suggest about the subject of the story? What do the students think they may learn from reading this story? Record students' predictions and expectations.

Tell students that the story is about a Spanish knight and priest named Ignatius Loyola.

Fact or Fiction?

All characters in the story are historical figures with the exception of the narrator who is fictional. Events are a matter of historical record.

Students will find sources for this story at the back of their book, on page 181.

Tie-in to History and Geography

The Council of Trent, the Catholic Reformation, and the Society of Jesus shared a common goal: to counteract the influence of Protestantism in the countries to which it had spread. The effects were mixed. Most of the German lands in which Luther worked remained Protestant. Bavaria and Austria were regained for Roman Catholicism by the end of the 1500s. The Wars of Religion between 1562 and 1598 reclaimed France for the Roman Catholic cause, although Protestants were tolerated until 1685. Poland and Bohemia also returned to Catholicism.

Have students study the map on page 55 to get a sense of which regions of Europe became primarily Protestant during the Reformation.

People and Terms to Know

Ignatius Loyola—(1491–1556) Spanish-born founder of the Catholic religious organization known as the Society of Jesus, or Jesuits. The Jesuits were important in helping the Catholic Church reform itself.

page—boy who served a knight as part of his own training for knighthood.

Castile—Spanish kingdom that joined with the kingdom of Aragón in 1479 to form a united Spain.

Holy Land—Palestine, the region where Jesus was born.

fasted—ate little or nothing, often for religious reasons.

hospice—house kept by monks that offered a place of rest for travelers.

Spiritual Exercises—famous book of readings, prayers, and meditations written by Ignatius Loyola.

Inquisition—court established by the Roman Catholic Church to find heretics and get rid of ideas that went against the Church's teachings.

(Tested vocabulary words used in the online vocabulary quiz are underlined.)

During Reading

Students can use the **Study Guide** on the next page to help them understand and enjoy the story and recognize its importance in history.

After Reading

Students can answer the **Questions to Consider** in the book as a way to deepen their interpretation of the selection.

1. What led Loyola to dedicate his life to the service of the Church?

2. Why did Loyola go back to school at the age of 33?

3. What role did the Society of Jesus play in European history?

4. How did the work and activities of the Jesuits differ from those of other religious orders?

Bibliography

Ignatius Loyola

James Janda. *Inigo: The Life of St. Ignatius Loyola for Young Readers* (1995). Inigo found God in all things. He founded the Society of Jesus, an order dedicated to many good works. Jesuits, as these men were called, teach and work in parishes, hospitals, prisons, and missions around the world. They all follow the example of their founder, St. Ignatius of Loyola. *Inigo* tells us about the life of this unique man, his triumphs, and his failures.

Mary Purcell. Image Books. *First Jesuit: St. Ignatius Loyola 1491–1556* (1965). The story of Ignatius of Loyola, the founder of the Jesuit order.

History of the Catholic Church

Martin E. Marty. *Christianity in the New World: from 1500 to 1800* (1984). An illustrated history of the Church.

Michael Pennock, James Hogan. *The Catholic Church Story* (1991). Gives an overview of the history of Christianity, with emphasis on the beliefs and institutions of the Catholic Church.

Religious Life

Margaret Mayo. *Brother Sun, Sister Moon: The Life and Stories of St. Francis* (2000). The story of St. Francis of Assisi, who rejected his wealthy background to lead a life of poverty, good works, and kindness to animals.

The History of Europe

Trevor Cairns. *The Birth of Modern Europe* (1975). Traces the history of Europe from 1500 to 1715, focusing on the roles played by religion and politics.

Name _____

From Soldier to Saint
by Walter Hazen

1. Why did the life of Ignatius Loyola change when he was 30?

_____

_____

_____

2. Why do you think that Loyola stayed in Manresa before going to Jerusalem?

_____

_____

_____

3. What were some of Loyola's ideas that attracted followers?

_____

_____

_____

4. Why does the narrator think that the Jesuits were successful in bringing people back to the Church?

_____

_____

_____

5. Essay Question

What is your opinion of Loyola's comment that "We ought always to be ready to believe that what seems to us white is black if the Church so defines it"?

Name _____

People and Terms to Know

This page lets you check your knowledge of the people and the terms used in "From Soldier to Saint." Find the best answer for each item. Then circle that answer.

1. This is a book of readings and prayers written by the head of the Jesuits.

   a. Ignatius Loyola

   b. Holy Land

   c. Spiritual Exercises

   d. Inquisition

2. Which is the best description of a hospice?

   a. place where sick people are treated

   b. cave in the hills

   c. place where monks live

   d. house where travelers could rest

3. Who was a Spanish knight who later became a priest and founded a religious order?

   a. Ignatius Loyola

   b. Castile

   c. Manresa

   d. Pope Paul III

4. This is the region where Jesus was born.

   a. Loyola

   b. Holy Land

   c. Spain

   d. Rome

5. Which term describes a Church court established to find and get rid of heretics and heretical ideas?

   a. Holy Court

   b. Holy Land

   c. Spiritual Exercises

   d. Inquisition

Answer Key

From Soldier to Saint
by Walter Hazen

After Reading

1. During his recuperation, the only books he had to read were the life of Christ and a book of lives of the saints. These books changed his way of thinking and made him want to be a priest.

2. He found that he couldn't become a priest unless he knew Latin, so he had to go to school to learn it.

3. Followers were attracted because Loyola believed in setting up schools and universities in places throughout the world.

4. Many other religious orders stayed in their monasteries and led lonely lives as monks. The Jesuits went out into the world as missionaries.

Study Guide

Answers will vary. Possible answers follow.

1. He was seriously injured in a battle and had a long period of recuperation.

2. Some students may suggest that he ran out of money and couldn't afford to get to Jerusalem. Others may say that he found something he was looking for in Manresa and felt that he was doing what he was supposed to do by living a very simple life and spending his days in prayer and service.

3. He had ideas about good works and wanted equal treatment for women.

4. He thought that they succeeded because they were dedicated to their cause and were well-educated and trained.

5. Essay Question Some students may realize that this was a time when many people believed that anything the Church said, whether it was about religion or the nature of the world, must be true. It was considered wrong to question anything that the Church said. Other students may say that this just gave the Church too much power and that people should use their own minds to figure out the truth. They might say that the Church should have to prove what they are saying if they are asking people to believe things that go against their instincts or feelings. Students should explain their answers.

Building Vocabulary

Answers: 1. c, 2. d, 3. a, 4. b, 5. d.

Cardinal Richelieu

BY BARBARA LITTMAN

Before Reading

Background

The story "Cardinal Richelieu" describes events in the life of Armand Jean du Plessis, cardinal of the Roman Catholic Church and duke of Richelieu. Armand was born in 1585, the youngest boy in a minor noble family. His father died when Armand was five. The threatened loss of an inherited bishopric made it was necessary for a member of the family to become a bishop as quickly as possible. The eldest son served in the military and the second was a monk, so the priesthood fell to Armand.

Armand was inclined to learning, had a talent for debate, and fancied the prospect of governing the lives of others. When he completed his studies, he was still below the legal age for consecration to the bishopric. He traveled to Rome to request a papal dispensation. Pope Paul V was captured by Armand's charm and he was ordained as both priest and bishop of the see of Luçon in 1607. He was 22.

Armand took over a diocese that had been ruined in the Wars of Religion (1562–1598), but he quickly asserted his authority. He was the first French bishop to implement the reforms decreed in the Council of Trent. As the story suggests, his primary goal in life was order, both spiritual and political.

France's king, Henry IV, had done much to strengthen the monarchy in France. Although he was a Huguenot, he converted to Catholicism, realizing that he could not rule Catholic France as a member of a minority religion. However, he issued a special order, the Edict of Nantes, guaranteeing some religious and political rights to citizens regardless of their religion.

When Henry was assassinated, his heir, Louis XIII, was only eight years old. Louis's mother, Marie dé Medici, ruled as regent. By now, Armand had entered the political arena, demonstrating both his intelligence and his support for royal authority. A favorite of Marie's, he was appointed advisor to Louis. After a brief revolt, Armand rose quickly to first minister. By that time, he had also been appointed cardinal of the Church.

In his search for order and the absolute control of the monarchy, Richelieu continued the work begun by Henry IV. The military strength of the nobles was a threat to the monarchy, so Richelieu ordered that any fortified castles that were not necessary for the defense of France must be torn down. Then he reduced the political power of the nobles and appointed governors of provinces who were both well-educated and supportive of a strong monarchy. He appointed regional administrators called *intendants*—middle-class people who had no interest in maintaining the power of the nobles. Some suggest that one role of these intendants was to monitor their regions for plots against the king.

Because Louis XIII was weak in both health and resolve, Richelieu literally ran the country from 1624 until his death in 1642. His actions against the Huguenots and later, in siding with Protestant nations against the Catholic Hapsburgs, are described in the story.

Preteaching the Story

To help students with background information, have them read page 13–14, "Religious Warfare" and "The Thirty Years' War." Pronounce the name of Richelieu (REESH•uh•LYOO). Use the story title as a starting point for students. What do they expect the story to be about? What do they think they may learn from reading this story? Record students' predictions and expectations.

Before they begin reading, help students to find and pronounce difficult names in the story, such as Huguenots (HYOO•guh•nahts), and Gustavus Adolphus (guh•STAY•vuhs uh•DAHL•fuhs).

Fact or Fiction?

The narrator is fictional, but the events in the story are historically accurate. Students will find sources for this story about the back of their book, on page 181.

Tie-in to History and Geography

The power of the Hapsburgs was a threat to the absolute monarchy that Richelieu wanted for France. The Thirty Years' War (1618–1648) provided an opportunity for him to strengthen France at the expense of the Hapsburgs. The war had begun before Richelieu became First Minister. It was an especially brutal war because many of the soldiers were mercenaries who fought for money rather than principles. Because they often went unpaid, they raided towns, stealing food and other goods.

Richelieu supported Protestant countries against the Hapsburgs, but believed that it was in France's best interest to prolong the war. France was not yet involved in the actual fighting and Richelieu reasoned that other nations would become weak while France remained strong. Germany took the brunt of the fire, disease, and plundering of the mercenaries. France eventually joined the fighting. By 1648, France had become the most powerful country in Europe. Have students study the map on page 55 and explain why France sided with the Protestant countries against Spain and the Hapsburgs of the Holy Roman Empire.

People and Terms to Know

Cardinal Richelieu (REESH•uh•LYOO)—(1585–1642) high official in the Catholic Church and chief minister of France under King Louis XIII. He was responsible for policies that eventually broke Hapsburg control of Europe.

Treaty of Westphalia—treaty that ended the Thirty Years' War in 1648. The Hapsburgs and the Holy Roman Empire were on one side, and a number of German princes backed by France, Sweden, and Denmark were on the other. The treaty weakened the Hapsburgs' hold on Europe, and France became the major power in Europe.

Hapsburg—powerful European ruling family. At the height of their power, the Hapsburgs controlled most of Europe, including Germany, and Spain and the Spanish colonies in the Americas. Almost all of the Holy Roman Emperors from 1438 on were Hapsburgs.

Huguenots (HYOO•guh•nahts)—French Protestant followers of John Calvin. Ever since the Edict of Nantes in 1598, they had had freedom of worship in France and the right to build towns and arm themselves for protection. Richelieu used a Protestant uprising as an excuse to capture their towns and take away their political rights.

dike—low wall built to prevent floods or to dam rivers.

Louis XIII—(1601–1643) king of France from 1610 to 1643. Basically, Louis let Richelieu, and after him Mazarin, run the country.

Gustavus Adolphus (guh•STAY•vuhs uh•DAHL•fuhs)—(1594–1632) king of Sweden 1611–1632. He defeated the Hapsburgs in three major battles and helped break their hold on Europe.

(Tested vocabulary words used in the online vocabulary quiz are underlined.)

During Reading

Use the **Study Guide** on the next page to help you understand and enjoy the story and recognize its importance in history.

After Reading

Answer the **Questions to Consider** in the book as a way to deepen your interpretation of the selection.

1. What were Cardinal Richelieu's most important goals?

2. What were the reasons the European powers fought the Thirty Years' War?

3. Why was Cardinal Richelieu willing to join with Protestant rulers to fight against Catholic countries, even though Richelieu and his king were Catholic?

4. How did the war make it possible for France to become a leader in Europe?

Bibliography

Cardinal Richelieu

Pat Glossop. *Cardinal Richelieu* (1990). A biography of the able seventeenth-century statesman who, for more than eighteen years, was the actual ruler of France during the reign of Louis XIII.

The Huguenots

Mary Casanova. *Curse of a Winter Moon* (2000). This historical novel presents a story about village superstition during the struggle between the Church and the Huguenots in France in the late 1500s. In sixteenth-century France, ruled by a Church that overtaxes peasants and burns heretics, Marius must postpone his apprenticeship to care for his six-year-old brother, whose birth took their mother's life, and who the villagers, backed by the Church, believe will become a "loup garou" — a werewolf.

G. A. Henty. *St. Bartholomew's Eve: A Tale of the Huguenot Wars* (1998). Cardinal Richelieu wages war on the Huguenots.

Thirty Years War

G. A. Henty. *The Lion of the North: A Tale of the Times of Gustavus Adolphus* (2000). A historical novel dealing with the first part of the Thirty Years' War.

G. A. Henty. *Won by the Sword: A Story of the Thirty Years' War* (2000). History of the Thirty Years' War.

French History

Bill Crider. *Muttketeer!* (1999). Locked out of school while Joe and his friends are inside, Wishbone imagines himself as D'Artagnan, a young seventeenth-century Frenchman who achieves his dream of becoming one of the prestigious musketeers who guard the king and his court.

Alexandre Dumas (translated by William Barrow). *The Three Musketeers* (1999). Alexandre Dumas's classic tale of adventure takes place in the France of King Louis XIII and Cardinal Richelieu.

Henry M. Schlesinger, Albert C. Gross. *Henry of Navarre* (1988). A biography of the French king who resolved religious conflict in his country, issued the Edict of Nantes, and made other important reforms before being assassinated.

Name _____

Cardinal Richelieu
by Barbara Littman

1. Who was Cardinal Mazarin and what was he doing at the beginning of the story?

_____

_____

_____

2. How did Richelieu defeat the Huguenots at La Rochelle?

_____

_____

_____

3. Why do you think that King Louis chose Richelieu over his mother?

_____

_____

_____

4. What did Richelieu accomplish by helping Gustavus Adolphus? Use the map on page 55 to help you answer the question.

_____

_____

_____

5. Essay Question

What do you think of Richelieu's actions in siding with the Protestants against the Catholics, even though he was a cardinal of the Catholic Church?

Name _____

People and Terms to Know

This page lets you check your knowledge of the people and the terms used in "Cardinal Richelieu." Find the best answer for each item. Then circle that answer.

1. Which Catholic family ruled much of Europe during the 1500s?

   a. Richelieu

   b. Louis XIII

   c. Hapsburg

   d. Adolphus

2. This person was a king of France during the 1600s.

   a. Cardinal Richelieu

   b. Louis XIII

   c. Hapsburg

   d. Gustavus Adolphus

3. Who sided with Protestant countries to make France strong?

   a. Cardinal Richelieu

   b. Louis XIII

   c. Hapsburg

   d. Gustavus Adolphus

4. Which is the best description of the Treaty of Westphalia?

   a. treaty that gave religious freedom to the Huguenots

   b. treaty that ended the battle of La Rochelle

   c. treaty that ended the Thirty Years' War

   d. treaty that made Gustavus Adolphus king of Sweden

5. This Swedish king agreed to protect the lands around the Baltic Sea.

   a. Richelieu

   b. Louis XIII

   c. Hapsburg

   d. Gustavus Adolphus

Answer Key

Cardinal Richelieu
by Barbara Littman

After Reading

1. He wanted a strong, unified France and loyalty to the crown.

2. Answers will vary. Students may suggest that the Hapsburgs wanted to keep their large empire and continue to rule, while the kings and leaders of now Protestant countries wanted to be free from the Emperor's rule and permitted to lead their own countries. They also wanted to be able to practice whatever religion they chose instead of being forced into Catholicism.

3. Richelieu believed that a strong monarchy would keep France strong and unified. He saw the end of the Hapsburg rule as the only way to achieve this goal. He believed he could win over the Hapsburgs by working with the Protestant countries.

4. Students' answers will vary. Students may recognize that the war weakened the Holy Roman Empire and prevented Spain and the rest of the Empire from uniting to take over France. Since France mainly contributed to the war with money, they didn't become weak from fighting as the other countries did.

Study Guide

Answers will vary. Possible answers follow.

1. He was the cardinal who succeeded Cardinal Richelieu and he was there to sign the Treaty of Westphalia at the end of the Thirty Years' War.

2. He cut off their supplies from both land and sea and eventually starved them into surrendering.

3. Students may suggest that Louis knew how much Richelieu had accomplished for France and thought it was more important than what his mother could do. Others may say that Louis didn't like Marie's attempts to control him and chose Richelieu, who supported the same goals.

4. Students should see that if the Hapsburgs were defending the land near the Baltics, they'd be too busy to attack France. Also the empire would be weakened while France remained strong.

5. **Essay Question** Students may recall that, at the time, church officials had a lot of political power. Richelieu never changed his position that political order is most important, so it was reasonable to do whatever had to be done to maintain that order. To him that meant keeping the monarchy strong. Other students may say that he betrayed his Catholic position by supporting Protestant countries against the Catholic Hapsburgs.

Building Vocabulary

Answers: **1.** c, **2.** b, **3.** a, **4.** c, **5.** d.

Text Pages 61–70

The Glorious Revolution

BY JUDY VOLEM

Before Reading

Background

The story "The Glorious Revolution" shifts to the effects of the Reformation in England. England had a tradition of resistance to the popes that went back to the 1300s. Protestant ideas had filtered into the country by the 1520s, but made few inroads until King Henry VIII decided that he wanted to divorce his wife and marry someone who would bear him a male heir.

Henry had once defended the Church so strongly that the pope had given him the title of "Defender of the Faith." Pope Clement VII could have granted Henry permission to divorce, but refused for political reasons. In 1529, Henry withdrew England from the Catholic Church and created a new church, the Church of England. Henry's objections were not philosophical, but merely political. Of course, Henry's church granted his divorce, and he went on to have a total of six wives.

By 1685, England had suffered through many years of religious conflict. Those in line for the throne were sometimes Protestant and sometimes Catholic and each new ruler supported his or her religion. During the reign of Charles II (1660–1685), Catholicism was tolerated. Two political parties, the Tories and the Whigs, developed. They disagreed about who should succeed Charles because he had no children. When Charles died in 1685, his brother James II came to the throne. James was Catholic and believed in absolute monarchy. He enraged both the Tories and the Whigs and frightened Protestants with his actions to ease life for Catholics. To make matters worse, in 1688, James and his wife Mary had a son who was raised Catholic. The Protestants feared a whole line of Catholic kings.

One of James's daughters, Mary II, had married William III, prince of Orange and ruler of the Netherlands. William had welcomed English aid in helping him check the growth of French power in Europe. An association had arisen between William and some of England's influential men. When James's actions became intolerable, they appealed to William to take over. His claim to the throne was supported by his marriage to James's daughter.

George Jeffreys was born of a Welsh noble family in about 1645. In 1677, he was appointed solicitor general to Charles II's brother James, then the duke of York. In 1678, Jeffreys prosecuted a number of Catholic conspirators and became known for ridiculing and bullying the defendants.

Despite his Protestantism and his role as a prosecutor of Catholics, Jeffreys became increasingly prominent in Charles's court. He supported James's succession to the throne and became Lord Chief Justice. He developed a reputation for convicting and executing rebels on the flimsiest of evidence. He also profited by extorting money from the victims.

When William of Orange overthrew James's government in the Glorious Revolution of 1688, Jeffreys tried to escape disguised as a sailor, but was arrested and died four months later in the Tower of London.

Preteaching the Story

Direct students to read pages 15–16, "Religious Conflict in England." Use the story title as a starting point for students. What do students expect the story to be about? What do students think they may learn from reading this story? Record students' predictions and expectations.

Explain that the story involves events that took place in England during the late 1600s. To help them read the story smoothly, pronounce Assizes (uh•SYZ•uhs). Explain that these are court sessions.

Fact or Fiction?

Nicholas Wood is a fictional character based on court clerks of the time. Other characters and events are historically accurate.

Students will find sources for this story at the back of their book, on page 181.

Tie-in to History and Geography

William did not automatically become king after the Glorious Revolution. He ran the government until Parliament met in early 1689. They decided that James's flight from the country was abdication and offered the crown jointly to William and his wife, Mary. At the same time, a Bill of Rights was passed. In accepting the crown, William and Mary also accepted a number of conditions placed on them by Parliament. The Bill of Rights barred Roman Catholics from the throne, abolished the right of the king to suspend laws, declared a standing army illegal in time of peace, and required frequent meetings of Parliament and free elections. The Bill of Rights supported John Locke's idea that government was a social contract between the king and his people, represented by Parliament.

People and Terms to Know

George Jeffreys—(c. 1645–1689) high level minister of law in England. The court sessions held by him after a revolt against James II resulted in so many executions they were called the "Bloody Assizes."

Henry VIII—(1491–1547) king of England from 1509 to 1547. Henry set up the Protestant Church of England.

Mary I—(1516–1558) queen of England from 1553 to 1558. She was the Catholic daughter of Henry VIII and his first wife, Catherine of Aragón, daughter of Ferdinand and Isabella of Spain.

Elizabeth I—(1533–1603) Protestant daughter of Henry VIII. His divorce to marry her mother, Anne Boleyn, began the Protestant Church of England. Elizabeth was queen of England from 1558 to 1603.

James II—(1633–1701) king of England from 1685 to 1688. James's Catholicism and the birth of his Catholic heir caused the Glorious Revolution.

treason—high crime against one's country. Spying and other acts of helping enemies are acts of treason.

Bloody Assizes (uh•SYZ•uhs)—trials of those involved in the duke of Monmouth's rebellion in 1685. *Assizes* means "court sessions."

Parliament—In England, the body of government that, with the king or queen, makes up the legislative (lawmaking) branch. It includes the House of Lords and the House of Commons.

Tower of London—famous prison in London.

William of Orange—(1650–1702) Protestant ruler in the Netherlands married to Mary, the daughter of England's King James II. Together they were invited by Parliament to become queen and king of England, Scotland, and Ireland. He ruled as William III from 1689 to 1702.

(Tested vocabulary words used in the online vocabulary quiz are underlined.)

During Reading

Students can use the **Study Guide** on the next page to help them understand and enjoy the story and recognize its importance in history.

After Reading

Students can answer the **Questions to Consider** in the book as a way to deepen their interpretation of the selection.

1. Why do you think that Judge George Jeffreys's behavior changed after his appointment by King James II?

2. Why did the seven bishops refuse to follow the king's orders?

3. What made the Glorious Revolution "glorious"?

4. What does this story show you about how rulers kept power and how they lost it?

Bibliography

Henry VIII

Crowell-Collier Press. *The Life and World of Henry VIII* (1970). The life and reign of the sixteenth-century English monarch who effected the separation of the English Church from Rome.

Robert Green. *King Henry VIII* (1998). A biography of the English monarch who challenged the Pope's authority, established a state religion, married six wives, and presided over the beginnings of the Renaissance in England.

John Van Duyn Southworth. *Monarch and Conspirators; the Wives and Woes of Henry VIII* (1973). Details the historical events of the reign of Henry VIII of England with emphasis on his six marriages.

Dorothy Turner. *Henry VIII* (1988). A brief account of the life of that complex personality, King Henry VIII of England.

Bill Yenne. *100 Men Who Shaped World History* (1994). Includes a biography of the life of Henry VIII.

The Glorious Revolution

Clarice Swisher. *The Glorious Revolution* (1996). Examines the events leading up to and the political legacy of the bloodless English overthrow of its monarchy.

English History

Dave Jackson, Neta Jackson. *The Queen's Smuggler* (1991). Sarah tries to smuggle a New Testament into England in order to save the life of William Tyndale, a man imprisoned for translating the Bible into English.

Scott O'Dell. *The Hawk That Dare Not Hunt by Day* (1988 paperback). Amid political turmoil and threats of plague, young Tom Barton accepts the risks of helping William Tyndale publish and smuggle into England the Bible he has translated into English.

Andy Thomson. *Morning Star of the Reformation* (1988). When young John of Wyoliffe arrives at Oxford University, he finds it a fascinating and perilous place. He and his companions discuss the political and religious issues of the day, and it is with his friends that he first shares his growing vision of an English Bible for all Englishmen to read. John paves the way for the theologians of the next century and opened hearts in preparation for the great Reformation itself.

Name _____

The Glorious Revolution
by Judy Volem

1. Why did Nicholas think that he'd made a big mistake taking the job as Jeffreys's clerk?

_____

_____

_____

2. Why were there so many religious problems in England during the 1500s and 1600s?

_____

_____

_____

3. Why were the trials known as the Bloody Assizes?

_____

_____

_____

4. How did James II go about bringing England under Catholic control?

_____

_____

_____

5. Essay Question
   Why do you think no one fought back when William of Orange invaded England?

Name _____

People and Terms to Know

This page lets you check your knowledge of the people and the terms used in "The Glorious Revolution." Find the best answer for each item. Then circle that answer.

1. This term refers to the British legislature.

   a. treason
   b. Bloody Assizes
   c. Parliament
   d. Council of Trent

2. This king started his own church in England.

   a. Henry VIII
   b. James II
   c. George Jeffreys
   d. William of Orange

3. This ruler was invited to invade England by Protestant leaders.

   a. Henry VIII
   b. James II
   c. George Jeffreys
   d. William of Orange

4. Which is the best definition of treason?

   a. crimes against one's country
   b. famous prison in London
   c. sessions of the court
   d. overthrowing the king

5. This king broke his promises about obeying the laws of England.

   a. Henry VIII
   b. James II
   c. George Jeffreys
   d. William of Orange

Answer Key

The Glorious Revolution
by Judy Volem

After Reading

1. Jeffreys had been ordered by the king to frighten and punish anyone who disagreed with Catholicism. He obeyed out of both loyalty and fear.
2. Students may suggest that James had gone too far in trying to force people to accept Catholicism. He had broken his word to obey the laws and had persecuted Protestants.
3. It was glorious because it happened without any violence. When William invaded, there was no one to fight back because James's troops abandoned him. No one was killed or injured in the revolution.
4. Students may suggest that rulers kept power by giving the people rights and freedom. They lost power when they tried to make the people do what they wanted and began to persecute them.

Study Guide

Answers will vary. Possible answers follow.
1. Jeffreys had become cruel and unfair after he carried out James's orders against the Protestants. Once James was gone and Jeffreys had been captured, there was no one left to protect Nicholas. People would have thought that he was as bad as Jeffreys because he worked as court clerk.
2. England had gone through many different Protestant and Catholic kings and queens since the time of Henry VIII. There were disagreements about which was better and whether the religion that the ruler believed in should be enforced for all the people.
3. Assizes are court sessions. During the trials of the supporters of the duke of Monmouth, hundreds of people were sentenced to hang or to be sold into slavery. There was much injustice and cruelty, so the sessions received the name of "bloody."
4. James broke the laws that he had promised to uphold. He listened to only Catholic advisors and removed Protestants from positions of power, replacing them with Catholics. Sometimes this meant killing innocent people.

5. Essay Question Some students may suggest that James's troops didn't like what the King had done any better than the other people and wanted to see James removed. Others may say that the soldiers knew they couldn't win because so many people supported William. They might end up fighting their own citizens. Students should support their ideas with reasons.

Building Vocabulary

Answers: **1.** c, **2.** a, **3.** d, **4.** a, **5.** b.

Man and Society: Four Views

BY JUDITH LLOYD YERO

Before Reading

Background

The story "Man and Society: Four Views" presents ideas of four of the greatest thinkers of the Age of Enlightenment, an intellectual movement during the 1600s and 1700s in which ideas about God, reason, nature, and humanity began to change. The key to Enlightenment thought was the use of reason and the celebration of man's power to understand the universe and improve his own life. The goals of the Enlightenment were knowledge, freedom, and happiness.

Ancient Greek philosophers, such as Plato and Aristotle, had been the first to develop the powers of reason. They had used their own intelligence to think about not only the order of nature but the workings of their own minds. When the Greek and Roman cultures gave way to Christianity, Christian thinkers also found uses for these ideas. However, they insisted that human understanding was less important than spiritual revelation and the truths of Christianity. Even if human beings used the evidence of their senses to figure something out, it must still pass the test of religious doctrine.

During the Renaissance and the Reformation, three movements weakened the power of the Church to dictate people's thoughts and actions. First, the Renaissance produced the successful experimental sciences of Sir Francis Bacon, Nicholas Copernicus, and Galileo, as well as the mathematical proofs of Descartes and Newton. Second, the Renaissance revived the notion of man's creative abilities—magnificent works of art and architecture springing from the same minds that were previously believed incapable of discerning the truth without Church guidance.

Third, the Reformation challenged the ultimate authority of the Roman Catholic Church itself. For each of these movements, the way to truth could be found in the application of human reason and creative genius. Eventually, this same rational thought was applied to religion itself. This led to deism—the belief that few religious truths were needed to know God and that those truths were available to any thinking person.

The Enlightenment produced the first theories of psychology and ethics. John Locke insisted that the mind of a newborn human was a *tabula rasa* (Latin), a "blank slate" upon which experience would write, shaping the individual personality. Religious teachings such as inborn goodness and original sin had no place in this view of the mind.

Thomas Hobbes had a more negative view, believing that man was motivated only by his drive for survival and the experience of pleasure. Again, these were seen as natural, rather than a reflection of a person's innate goodness or evil. Rather than mirroring an "eternal order," the state was now seen as a mutually beneficial arrangement aimed at protecting man's natural rights and self-interest.

As ideas about "social contracts" were put forth, it became obvious that many existing governments bore little resemblance to such a contract. They were authoritarian and hierarchical, based on the desires of the leader rather than the needs of the people. The thinking of Locke, Rousseau, Montesquieu, and later, Voltaire and Thomas Jefferson, led to a reappraisal of these governments and eventually to reform in England and revolution in America and France.

Preteaching the Story

Have students read pages 17–19, "The Enlightenment" and "Major Thinkers of the Enlightenment." Explain that each of the thinkers was trying to explain the nature of man and why people agree to be governed. Use the story title and illustration as a starting point for students. Ask students what they think they may learn from reading this story. Record students' predictions and expectations.

To help students with difficult pronunciation, tell them that the story is about four great thinkers and their ideas. Pronounce the names of Montesquieu (MAHN•tuh•skyoo) and Rousseau (roo•SOH).

Fact or Fiction?

Everything in the story is based on the actual words of the four Enlightenment philosophers. Their words have been paraphrased, but the ideas are intact.

Students will find sources for this story at the back of their book, on page 182.

Tie-in to History and Geography

Using the Time Line on page 26, have students compare the dates of the four philosopher's lives with the dates of events they've read about in other stories in this book. Remind them that the Renaissance with its great works of art was also taking place during the 1400s and 1500s.

Help students to see how the discovery of the Americas, the religious Reformations, and startling scientific discoveries all contributed to making people rethink their old beliefs. They were no longer willing to allow the Church scholars to tell them what to believe about nature and their own abilities. The next logical step was to question the monarchies and other forms of government that they had lived under and accepted. Ask students what they think might happen when people (1) realize that they have the right and ability to decide their own lives; and (2) realize that these rights and abilities have been denied them by their rulers.

People and Terms to Know

Enlightenment—European philosophical movement in the 1700s that emphasized the use of reason to examine accepted ideas. It encouraged many reforms and influenced the American and French Revolutions.

Thomas Hobbes—(1588–1679) English philosopher. He argued that people and their government were held together by a social contract. In this contract, people had agreed to give up freedom in order to have protection. He thought a ruler should have absolute power.

John Locke—(1632–1704) English philosopher. He believed that people have a right to end a government that doesn't protect a person's rights to life, liberty, and possessions. Locke's ideas had great influence on America's founding fathers.

Baron Charles de Montesquieu (MAHN•tuh•skyoo)—(1689–1755) French writer who examined different forms of government. He recommended the separation of powers, as well as checks and balances. James Madison argued for using these ideas in the U.S. Constitution.

Jean-Jacques Rousseau (roo•SOH)—(1712–1778) French philosopher. He said that people were born equal and argued that society made people unequal. His ideas influenced the leaders of the French Revolution.

(Tested vocabulary words used in the online vocabulary quiz are underlined.)

During Reading

Use the **Study Guide** on the next page to help you understand and enjoy the story and recognize its importance in history.

After Reading

Answer the **Questions to Consider** in the book as a way to deepen your interpretation of the selection.

1. Who, in your opinion, has the best ideas about why people join in a society and how they should be governed? Why?

2. What evidence can you think of for and against Hobbes's argument that people are by nature selfish and violent?

3. How does separating the powers of government protect the people in a society?

4. When government leaders don't use their power well, what rights do you think people should have?

Bibliography

Age of Enlightenment

John M. Dunn. *The Enlightenment* (1999). Discusses the origins of the Enlightenment along with the important figures of the movement and their influence.

Jonathan Swift (retold by James Dunbar). *Gulliver's Travels* (2000). Jonathan Swift, like other Enlightenment thinkers, had strong views about the society of his time. His hero, Gulliver, travels to many strange places, learning things about his own society and about human nature.

Enlightenment Thinkers

John Locke. *The Second Treatise on Civil Government* (paperback 1982). A translation of Locke's influential document.

Michael Pollard. *Thinkers* (1991). Biographical capsules of significant individuals who have influenced the world of ideas, from Plato to Nelson Mandela.

John W. Selfridge. *Thomas Jefferson: The Philosopher President* (1991). As a young revolutionary armed with knowledge and conviction, Thomas Jefferson helped forge a nation dedicated to freedom.

Jeremy Weate. *Young Person's Guide to Philosophy: "I think, Therefore I Am"* (1998). Introduces over 25 of the world's greatest philosophers and presents a simple version of the tenets of philosophy.

John Tyerman Williams. *Pooh and the Philosophers: In Which It Is Shown That All of Western Philosophy Is Merely a Preamble to Winnie-The-Pooh* (1996). The title speaks for itself!

European History

Katherine Sturtevant. *At the Sign of the Star* (2000). Meg Moore is a bright, independent, twelve-year-old who lives in London, England, in the 1670s. When her father remarries, she begins a battle of wits with her stepmother. This historical novel creates a richly detailed picture of Meg's world.

Name _____

Man and Society: Four Views
by Judith Lloyd Yero

1. Why, according to Hobbes, do people in a society get into arguments?

_____

_____

_____

2. Why did Hobbes think that it was important to keep people from fighting?

_____

_____

_____

3. Why does John Locke believe that people agree to form a society?

_____

_____

_____

4. What did Rousseau think was the greatest problem in society?

_____

_____

_____

5. Essay Question

In what ways does the government of the United States use the ideas of Baron Montesquieu?

Name _____

People and Terms to Know

This page lets you check your knowledge of the people and the terms used in "Man and Society: Four Views." Find the best answer for each item. Then circle that answer.

1. This person thought that different parts of the government should be responsible for making and enforcing laws.

    a. Thomas Hobbes

    b. John Locke

    c. Baron Montesquieu

    d. Jean-Jacques Rousseau

2. Which of the following is the best description of the Enlightenment?

    a. movement that marked the beginning of Protestantism

    b. movement that brought great scientific development

    c. movement that stressed the use of reason to examine ideas

    d. movement that denied people the right to rule themselves

3. Which of these people thought that a strong monarch was necessary to keep people from fighting?

    a. Thomas Hobbes

    b. John Locke

    c. Baron Montesquieu

    d. Jean-Jacques Rousseau

4. Which of these men was a French philosopher whose ideas contributed to the French Revolution?

    a. Thomas Hobbes

    b. John Locke

    c. Baron Montesquieu

    d. Jean-Jacques Rousseau

5. This person believed that people had the right to end a government that didn't protect their rights.

    a. Thomas Hobbes

    b. John Locke

    c. Baron Montesquieu

    d. Jean-Jacques Rousseau

Man and Society: Four Views
by Judith Lloyd Yero

After Reading

1. Answers will vary. Students may select any of the four but should support their choice with reasons.

2. Some students might point to all the crime and violence in society as evidence that people are selfish and violent by nature. They may say that many people help one another and do volunteer work as evidence against Hobbes's argument. There are many reasonable answers that students might give.

3. If the same person makes the laws, enforces the laws, and sits in judgment over people who break the laws, it's too easy to abuse that power and take away an individual's rights. When each branch of government has a different responsibility, it can stop other branches from doing something that will hurt the people.

4. Answers will vary. Some students may believe that the people have the right to remove the leaders from office. Other students may remember that not all countries are democracies. For example, it would be hard for the people to remove the Queen of England. Other leaders, such as dictators, hold so much power over the people that only a revolution can get rid of them.

Study Guide

Answers will vary. Possible answers follow.

1. Hobbes said that there were three reasons. Firstly, they compete and try to invade one another's territory to gain an advantage. Secondly, they don't trust one another and attack out of fear of what others might do to them. Thirdly, they go to war for glory or to become famous.

2. He said that when they are fighting, they don't have time to do anything productive—to build, or to study science, the arts, or literature. Also, they live in constant fear.

3. Locke said that people form societies to help one another protect their lives, liberties, and property. They join to have comfortable, safe, and peaceful lives and to get protection against foreigners.

4. Rousseau said that the door was opened to arguments, crime, and war the first time someone came up with the idea of private property and other people accepted the idea. He thought that the idea of private property had started more trouble than any other idea in history.

5. **Essay Question** Some students may say that the American people have the right to elect their own representatives and remove (impeach) politicians who don't act properly. They may also point to the three branches of government as an example of separation of powers, which creates checks and balances. All reasonable answers should be accepted.

Building Vocabulary

Answers: 1. c, 2. c, 3. a, 4. d, 5. b.

Text Pages 82–91

Voltaire and Frederick the Great

BY MARIANNE McCOMB

Before Reading

Background

"Voltaire and Frederick the Great" describes a portion of the life of the great Enlightenment thinker and writer François-Marie Arouet. Arouet is better known as Voltaire. During the 1700s, Voltaire was a recognized French *philosophe*, a combination philosopher and social critic.

Born in 1694 of bourgeois origins, young Arouet was raised by his grandfather. He attended a Jesuit college in Paris, where he enjoyed literature, the theater, and the social life. However, the religious instruction was not to his liking and he abandoned the study of law. Despite his reputation as the wit of Parisian society, Arouet was serious-minded and set about learning the accepted literary forms. After writing a successful play, he vowed to become the Virgil of France and took the name of Voltaire.

Voltaire traveled to England, where he learned English and spent several years meeting with England's great men of letters. He studied English thought and literature and firmly believed that it was the personal liberty of the English that had given England its economic advantages and victories over France. He was particularly impressed with Shakespearean theater, although he was shocked at its "barbarism."

Returning to France in about 1729, Voltaire attacked everything he believed to be superstition or pretense. His many writings, which included plays, histories, essays, poems, and stories, demonstrate not only his critical capacity but also his wit and satirical ability. In fact, his tendency to satirize leaders of the day resulted in a need to move about Europe quite often.

He became a harsh critic of prejudice, bigotry, and particularly, religious intolerance. However, his satirical condemnation of the problems he saw in French society made even his supporters uneasy. On the one hand, his writings were praised for their brilliance, but he was frustrated that the French people preferred the sentimental comedies of the day to his more thought-provoking work.

Throughout his life, Voltaire kept up an enormous correspondence with other philosophes, kings and queens, actors and actresses, and literary figures of the day. No subject of importance was beyond his comment, from political ideas to the Italian hypothesis of spontaneous generation. Reactions to Voltaire's ideas were rarely moderate. After 1800, he was even declared responsible for the French Revolution. Although many of his works have been forgotten, his stories and letters are still read and admired for their clarity of thought.

Voltaire was a master of one-liners such as "Judge a man by his questions rather than his answers." A line often attributed to him—"I disapprove of what you say, but I will defend to the death your right to say it"—beautifully illustrates Voltaire's belief in tolerance. Unfortunately, he probably never said it, for it is found in none of his writings.

Preteaching the Story

Direct students to pages 18–19, "Major Thinkers of the Enlightenment" and have them review the items on Voltaire (vohl•TAIR). Use the story title and illustration as a starting point for students. Ask students what they already know about Frederick the Great. What do they think this story is about? What do they think they will learn from it? Record students' predictions and expectations.

Tell students that the story is about a great thinker from the Age of Enlightenment. Read and discuss one or two of Voltaire's statements from page 91 and tell them that he was known for his witty satire—his ability to make fun of some of the things that people did or thought.

Fact or Fiction?

The people and events mentioned in the story are part of historical record. Students will find sources for this story at the back of their book, on page 182.

Tie-in to History and Geography

In the Middle Ages, the Hohenzollern family had ruled a small territory in southern Germany. During the Reformation, the Protestant Hohenzollerns seized Church lands in their territories. By the end of the Thirty Years' War in 1648, they ruled several widely scattered territories in Germany, including Prussia bordering the Baltic Sea.

The first king of Prussia, Frederick I, tried to imitate the French court of Louis XIV. His son and successor, Frederick William I, disliked French ways and got rid of the luxury when he became king in 1713. He worried because his own son and successor, Frederick, had little interest in either military life or government service. Instead, he wrote poetry, played the flute, and read philosophy. Young Frederick was particularly influenced by the writings of Voltaire.

At one point, young Frederick even tried to flee the country with a friend. His father captured them and forced Frederick to watch as his friend was executed. Frederick William I needn't have worried because young Frederick went on to become an even stronger ruler than his father. His intelligence and dedication to expanding the territory and prestige of Prussia resulted in his being called Frederick the Great.

Show students a map of Europe after the Thirty Years' War and have them locate Prussia.

People and Terms to Know

Voltaire (vohl•TAIR)—(1694–1778) pen name of François-Marie Arouet, a French writer, historian, and philosopher.

Frederick II of Prussia—(1712–1786) third king of Prussia, who ruled from 1740 to 1786. Frederick the Great, as he was called, made Prussia the strongest military power in Europe during the 1700s.

Bastille (ba•STEEL)—famous prison in Paris, France.

freedom of the press—freedom of writers and newspapers to publish their ideas and views without government control.

allies—partners, usually by treaty. Allies often join forces to fight a common enemy.

(Tested vocabulary words used in the online vocabulary quiz are underlined.)

During Reading

Use the **Study Guide** on the next page to help you understand and enjoy the story and recognize its importance in history.

After Reading

Answer the **Questions to Consider** in the book as a way to deepen your interpretation of the selection.

1. What kind of man was Voltaire?

2. What was Voltaire's idea about the purpose of life?

3. Why would Voltaire's ideas cause trouble among the people of the 1700s?

4. Why did Frederick the Great admire Voltaire?

5. Would you have wanted to be Voltaire's friend if you were Frederick?

Bibliography

Voltaire

François-Marie Arouet Voltaire. *Zadig L'Ingenu, Vol. 1* (1978). A translation of two "philosophical tales," the first hitting out at the clergy and Catholic dogma, the second a thinly veiled attack on the powers-that-be.

François Marie Arouet de Voltaire. *Candide* (1978). *Candide* is the story of a gentle man who, though pummeled and slapped in every direction by fate, clings desperately to the belief that he lives in "the best of all possible worlds." Voltaire's most celebrated work.

Bill Yenne. *100 Men Who Shaped World History* (1994). Includes a biography of the life of Voltaire.

Frederick the Great

Mary Kittredge. *Frederick the Great* (1987). A biography of the eighteenth-century Prussian king whose firm government and military exploits earned him the title of "enlightened despot."

Bill Yenne. *100 Men Who Shaped World History* (1994). Includes a biography of the life of Frederick the Great.

France in the 1700s

Aliki. *The King's Day: Louis XIV of France* (1989). A day in the life of France's King Louis XIV, focusing on the elaborate ceremonies which took place when he dressed in the morning, ate his meals, conducted affairs of state, entertained, and finally, when he prepared to go to bed at night.

Freedom of the Press

J. Edward Evans. *Freedom of the Press* (1990). Beginning with a discussion of freedom of expression in ancient Greece and during the Middle Ages, Evans then looks at the American press since colonial days, covering such topics as censorship, libel, and pornography.

Name _____

Voltaire and Frederick the Great
by Marianne McComb

1. Why do you think that Voltaire kept up a correspondence with young Prince Frederick?

_____

_____

_____

2. How did Voltaire make his feelings about freedom and tolerance known to the people of Europe?

_____

_____

_____

3. Why did Voltaire stay in Prussia even though he didn't agree with everything that Frederick was doing?

_____

_____

_____

4. What were some of the reasons that Frederick finally broke off his friendship with Voltaire?

_____

_____

_____

5. Essay Question
   If you had been Voltaire, how would you have dealt with the problem of Frederick's poetry? Would you have told him that the poems were bad, tried to help him write better ones, or lied to him to keep his favor? Explain your answer.

Name _____

People and Terms to Know

This page lets you check your knowledge of the people and the terms used in "Voltaire and Frederick the Great." Find the best answer for each item. Then circle that answer.

1. Which of the following describes the liberty of writers or journalists to say what they want without government control?

   a. allies

   b. truce

   c. freedom of the Bastille

   d. freedom of the press

2. This person was a French philosopher and writer who believed in freedom of thought and religion.

   a. Voltaire

   b. Frederick II of Prussia

   c. Maupertuis

   d. Maria Theresa

3. Which term describes a prison in Paris, France?

   a. allies

   b. truce

   c. Bastille

   d. Tower of London

4. Which term refers to countries that agree to fight together against a common enemy?

   a. allies

   b. truce

   c. Bastille

   d. empires

5. Which of these people was a great king and also a poet?

   a. Voltaire

   b. Frederick II of Prussia

   c. Maupertuis

   d. Maria Theresa

Answer Key

Voltaire and Frederick the Great
by Marianne McComb

After Reading

1. Answers will vary. Some students may say that he was a brilliant thinker, clever and witty, or a serious person who believed in freedom of thought and religion. Others may say that he was vain, overly fond of luxury, or sarcastic. Answers should reflect an overall impression rather than just one or two adjectives.

2. Voltaire said that the purpose of life was to achieve happiness by knowing the arts and sciences and not spending your life trying to get to heaven.

3. Voltaire criticized the leaders who spent their time going to war and trying to build empires. He made fun of the actions of powerful leaders and this got him in trouble.

4. Voltaire was cultured, wise, and very popular. These were things that Frederick wanted to be. Some students may suggest that Frederick wanted Voltaire around so that he could become more like him.

5. Answers will vary. Some students may say that if they were young and inexperienced, they would want to learn from someone like Voltaire. Others may say that Voltaire was too proud and unpleasant, and they wouldn't have like him. Students should support their answers with reasons.

Study Guide

Answers will vary. Possible answers follow.

1. Students may suggest that Voltaire was flattered by Frederick's words and kept up the correspondence so that he would continue to get such words of praise. Others may suggest that he really wanted to help Frederick.

2. Voltaire published his ideas in pamphlets that were spread among the people of Europe.

3. When Voltaire visited Frederick's court, he lived a luxurious life. He had servants, a large salary, and many Prussian nobles who hung on his every word.

4. Voltaire still made Frederick feel like a student, even though he was a king. Voltaire told Frederick that his poems were worthless and insulted Maupertuis, a man that Frederick had appointed head of the Berlin Academy of Sciences. He made Frederick the laughing stock of Europe.

5. **Essay Question** Some students would suggest that Voltaire was too blunt and could have found some good things to say about the poetry rather than saying it should be destroyed. Other students may say that Voltaire should have suggested ways that Frederick could make his poetry better. Still others may say that Voltaire's life was so good that he should have kept his mouth shut about how bad the poetry was. Students should defend their choices with good reasons.

Building Vocabulary

Answers: 1. d, 2. a, 3. c, 4. a, 5. b.

At the Salon of Madame Geoffrin

BY STEPHEN FEINSTEIN

Before Reading

Background

Many of the famous *philosophes*—philosophers and social theorists—came from or were drawn to France. During the Age of Enlightenment, it was common for well-known hostesses to set up salons—gatherings of the social, political, and cultural elite. Accompanied by lavish entertainment and food, the philosophes could meet and discuss their ideas.

One hostess whose salons were famous was Madame Marie-Thérèse Geoffrin. She held her salons in the Hôtel de Ramouille in Paris. They became an international meeting place of artists and men of letters from 1749 to 1777, when Madame Geoffrin died.

Madame Geoffrin was the daughter of a valet. She married a rich member of the newly influential bourgeoisie with whom she had little in common. Madame Geoffrin was naturally intelligent, sensitive, and an excellent listener—all of which made her an ideal hostess for a salon. She inherited the salon of a previous hostess and gave it added respectability. Madame Geoffrin was a generous hostess to her guests and a motherly patron to her proteges, offering them both criticism and advice. She ran her salons with strict rules. Neither religion nor politics were allowed as topics of discussion.

As the story suggests, she kept the artists of the day separated from the writers. Madame Geoffrin's salon was also a meeting place for the Encyclopedists—those who contributed articles for a collection of ideas from the Enlightenment. The word encyclopedia comes from the Greek meaning "general education."

Great writers of the day all contributed articles to the French *Encyclopédie*. The writers were free to express their ideas without censorship. In addition to covering every subject, including the sciences, writers often criticized what they saw as flawed in society, such as the church, the government, the slave trade, torture, taxes, and war.

Philosopher Denis Diderot, aided by mathematician Jean D'Alembert, edited the *Encyclopédie* with generous support from Madame Geoffrin. Although Diderot had begun by translating a previously published English encyclopedia into French, he soon changed its nature, broadening the topics that it covered and turning it into a sounding board for revolutionary and radical opinion.

The first edition in 28 volumes was published between 1751 and 1772. Both conservative churchmen and government officials opposed its publication. They frowned on any work critical of their practices. The Church succeeded in censoring some of the volumes and suppressing others. In 1759, the *Encyclopédie* was formally condemned. This did not stop people across Europe from buying the *Encyclopédie*, reading it, and adopting many of the ideas that it contained.

Preteaching the Story

Begin with the story title. Pronounce the name of Madame Geoffrin (ZHAW•fruhn). Have students study the picture and its caption. Ask what they think a salon might be. What do students think that they might learn from the story? Record students' predictions and expectations. To help the students, tell them that the story is about a number of French writers and artists who lived during the Enlightenment, including Denis Diderot (DEE•duh•ROH), François Boucher (boo•SHAY) and Claude-Adrien Helvétius (hel•VEE•shuhs).

Fact or Fiction?

Henri and Etienne are fictional characters. The description of Paris in 1750 and the events and people at the salon are historically accurate. Criticism of the Church was popular during the Enlightenment. However, Madame Geoffrin forbade discussion of either religion or politics at her salon. She may have felt that those topics would degrade high-level discussion of ideas into emotional arguments.

Students will find sources for this story at the back of their book, on page 182.

Tie-in to History and Geography

Madame Geoffrin's salons took place during the reign of France's Louis XV. His grandfather, King Louis XIV, had brought France to a position of political, intellectual and artistic greatness. Unfortunately, Louis XV had little of his grandfather's skill and vision. He was lazy and lacked self-confidence. His government split into factions of scheming ministers and courtiers. Louis separated himself from the court and entertained himself with a series of mistresses. Several of them exerted considerable political influence. From 1745 until her death in 1764, Louis's official mistress was Jeanne-Antoinette Poisson—Madame Pompadour. Louis enjoyed the arts. Together with Madame Pompadour's brother, they built some of the most spectacular buildings in France. Louis and Jeanne patronized many forms of decorative arts. Painters, sculptors, furniture makers, and craftsmen all worked at the court. The famous porcelain factory at Sèvres was built during this time. Despite the military losses in the Seven Years' War and the loss of Canada to the English, all blamed on Madame Pompadour, this was probably the highest point in French culture.

Madame Pompadour was also a protector of authors, particularly the editor of the Encyclopédie, Denis Diderot. Unfortunately, Louis did not share her interest in literature and generally disliked intellectuals.

People and Terms to Know

Madame Geoffrin (ZHAW•fruhn)—Marie-Thérèse Geoffrin (1699–1777), wealthy French woman who hosted gatherings known as *salons* in Paris. There important philosophers, writers, and artists gathered to share ideas.

salon—regular gathering of notable people of social or intellectual distinction.

Denis Diderot (DEE•duh•ROH)—(1713–1784) French writer and encyclopedist. Diderot's 28-volume *Encyclopedia* (1751–1772) was a famous work of the Enlightenment that helped to shape the reason-based thinking of the time. *Monsieur* is French for "Mister."

François Boucher (boo•SHAY)—(1703–1770) French painter. His elegant but somewhat artificial work was very popular in this time.

Claude-Adrien Helvétius (hel•VEE•shuhs)—(1715–1771) French philosopher and conversationalist. He was the wealthy host of a group of Enlightenment thinkers known as *Philosophes*.

(Tested vocabulary words used in the online vocabulary quiz are underlined.)

During Reading

Students can use the **Study Guide** on the next page to help them understand and enjoy the story and recognize its importance in history.

After Reading

Students can answer the **Questions to Consider** in the book as a way to deepen their interpretation of the selection.

1. Why did Etienne begin to worry on the way to Madame Geoffrin's house?

2. What is Diderot's complaint about Boucher's paintings?

3. What didn't Madame Geoffrin invite artists to her salon the same day she invited writers and philosophers?

4. Why was Etienne shocked by the ideas of Helvétius?

5. If you were one of the guests of Madame Geoffrin, what would you have said?

Bibliography

France in the 17th and 18th Centuries

Janet and Isaac Asimov. *Norby and the Queen's Necklace* (1986). Fourteen-year-old Jeff Wells and his robot friend Norby are suddenly transported back to 1785 in France, where they become involved with a priceless necklace and royal politics.

James Barter. *The Palace of Versailles* (1998). Describes the building of the extravagant palace at Versailles in its historical context, particularly as a reflection of the personality and influence of Louis XIV.

Pierre L. Horn. *King Louis XIV* (1986). Presents the life of the seventeenth-century French monarch known as the "Sun King."

Time-Life Books. *What Life Was Like During the Age of Reason: France, A.D. 1660–1800* (1999). Narrative and pictures of life during the Enlightenment.

French History

Ethel Caro Gofen. *France* (1992). An overview of the geography, history, government, culture, and people of France.

Richard Ingham. *France* (2000). Examines the land, people, culture, and history of France and discusses its current state of affairs and place in the world.

Don Nardo. *France* (2000). Describes the geography, plants, animals, history, economy, language, sports, arts, religions, culture, and people of France.

Roseline NgCheong-Lum, Ayesha Ercelawn. *France* (1999). An overview of France, discussing its history, geography, government, economy, culture, and relationship with North America.

Name _____

At the Salon of Madame Geoffrin
by Stephen Feinstein

1. What would Etienne rather have been doing? Why?

_____

_____

_____

2. What interested Madame Geoffrin?

_____

_____

_____

3. What did Diderot include in his _Encyclopedia_ beside art?

_____

_____

_____

4. Why do you think that several of the guests believed that the Church having too much power in France was a bad thing?

_____

_____

_____

5. Essay Question
How do you think that ideas can be "food for thought"?

Name _____

People and Terms to Know

This page lets you check your knowledge of the people and the terms used in "At the Salon of Madame Geoffrin." Find the best answer for each item. Then circle that answer.

1. Which of the following was a famous French artist?

   a. Madame Geoffrin
   b. Denis Diderot
   c. François Boucher
   d. Claude-Adrien Helvétius

2. Who worked on an encyclopedia that contained information about many different subjects?

   a. Madame Geoffrin
   b. Denis Diderot
   c. François Boucher
   d. Claude-Adrien Helvétius

3. Which is the best definition of the word salon as it is used in this story?

   a. shop where people get their hair done
   b. regular meeting of notable people
   c. place where people go to argue about religion
   d. place where a person has to wear a wig and carry a cane

4. This person invited people to a gathering of writers, philosophers, or artists.

   a. Madame Geoffrin
   b. Denis Diderot
   c. François Boucher
   d. Claude-Adrien Helvétius

5. Which person was a French philosopher and conversationalist who thought that the Church was too powerful in France?

   a. Madame Geoffrin
   b. Denis Diderot
   c. François Boucher
   d. Claude-Adrien Helvétius

Answer Key

At the Salon of Madame Geoffrin
by Stephen Feinstein

After Reading
1. Henri told him that people at the salon discussed the latest ideas of the day. In addition to being dressed in an unfamiliar way, Etienne was from the country and didn't know about these ideas. He wasn't sure he'd know what to say.
2. Diderot said that the artist didn't know anything about delicacy, honesty, innocence, and simplicity. He claimed that the artist had never really seen nature.
3. She felt that only artists would understand what other artists were saying and felt it best not to mix artists with the writers and philosophers.
4. Helvétius was criticizing the Catholic Church and Etienne was a good Catholic.
5. Answers will vary. Students should recognize that they would be expected to comment about ideas rather than simply "making conversation."

Study Guide
Answers will vary. Possible answers follow.
1. He had just arrived in Paris from his home in the country and was anxious to see the sights of the city.
2. Politics, art, literature, and religion all interested Madame Geoffrin, which is why she chose to spend her time with men knowledgeable in these subjects.
3. He included literature, politics, economics, religion, and ethics.
4. Students might recall the problems that had been caused in England over the connection between religion and government. If the Catholic Church had a lot of power over the government, leaders of the Church could make things difficult for anyone who didn't share their religious beliefs.

5. **Essay Question** Some students may say that ideas are food for the mind just as meat and potatoes are food for the body. Ideas can be "chewed" and "digested." Some ideas are "distasteful." Accept any answer that is reasonable and draws a comparison between ideas and food.

Building Vocabulary
Answers: 1. c, 2. b, 3. b, 4. a, 5. d.

Catherine the Great

BY CAROLE POPE

Before Reading

Background

The story "Catherine the Great" takes place in Russia during Catherine's reign as empress from 1762 to 1796. Catherine was born Sophie Frederike Auguste and was a princess of a small German state. She had come to Russia at the age of 15 to be the bride of Russia's future heir, Peter III. It was then that she took the name of Catherine.

Even before he succeeded to the crown, Peter, who was mentally challenged and very pro-Prussian, managed to alienate not only his wife but also the politically powerful court elite. After he succeeded Empress Elizabeth, his popularity declined even more when he reversed her foreign policy, made peace with Prussia, and withdrew from the Seven Years' War. Even his actions to relieve Russian nobles of their obligation to serve the state won him no friends. He offended the Russian Orthodox Church by trying to force it to adopt Lutheran practices and alienated the imperial guards, threatening to disband them. His treatment of Catherine turned the members of Russian society against him.

Catherine also suspected that he was planning to divorce her. It was therefore easy for Catherine, with the support of the senators, high officials, and officers of the imperial guard, to overthrow Peter. He had been emperor for only about six months.

Catherine had lived in Russia for more than half her life by that time. She was familiar with intrigue and the struggle for power that had been ongoing since her arrival. She read contemporary literature, especially the French *Encyclopédie* and German writings on law. When she seized power at the age of 33, she was therefore prepared for her long reign of more than 30 years.

Catherine described herself as "a philosophe on the throne." In 1767, she prepared a document known as the "Instruction of Catherine the Great." In it, she recommended liberal, humanitarian political theories as the basis of government reform and the preparation of a new legal code. The Instruction maintained that all people should be considered equal before the law and that law should protect rather than burden the public. Catherine said that the law should forbid only those things that directly harmed other individuals or the community. She disapproved of capital punishment, torture, and serfdom. However, she also upheld the principle of absolutism, maintaining that all political power should be held by an autocrat subject to no law.

The Instruction was written as a guide for the legislators who were considering internal reform. It had little effect and no reforms or new legal codes were agreed upon. Although Catherine made no further effort to implement her ideas, they did form the basis of much Russian political thought.

Although Catherine supported the arts, science, literature, and theater, these had little meaning in the lives of the Russian people. They were generally unschooled and lived in great poverty. She did encourage the nobles to become more Westernized. Unfortunately, this took them even more out of touch with the common people.

Preteaching the Story

Use the story title as a starting point for students. Have students study the picture and read its caption. What do they think an empress would have to do to be called "great"? Ask students what they think the story might be about. What do students expect to learn from the story? Record students' predictions and expectations.

Fact or Fiction?

The narrator is a fictional character. The people and events in the story are historically accurate.

Students will find sources for this story at the back of their book, on page 182.

Tie-in to History and Geography

What made Catherine "great" were her expansionist policies. Although there were many rivers in Russia, during the cold winter months, seaports froze and Russia became landlocked. Since the days of Peter the Great, Russia had been trying to solve the problem. One of Peter's major goals was to acquire warm-water ports on the Black Sea. The Ottoman Empire controlled all the land between the Black Sea and the Mediterranean. In order to defeat the Turks, Peter needed strong allies and a much stronger, more efficient Russia.

Peter encountered problems because people of Russia spoke many different languages and many of them lived in isolated areas of the huge country. Peter did succeed in making Russia into a great power, but it took the efforts of Catherine to finally gain access to the Black Sea.

In a successful war against the Turks, she finally succeeded in gaining territory that could give Russia access to the Mediterranean. In addition to this important addition, Catherine also added a large share of Poland to her territory. By forcing Russia's borders well into central Europe, Russia became a player in the European balance of power.

Have students study a map of Russia during the time of Peter the Great and through the reign of Catherine. Help them to understand how important the acquisition of a warm-water seaport was to Russia's economy.

People and Terms to Know

Catherine II—(1729–1796) German-born princess who became known as Catherine the Great. She was married to Peter III and ruled Russia from June 1762 until her death. After Peter the Great, she is regarded a Russia's greatest ruler.

Grigory Orlov (grih•GOHR•ee uhr•LOF)—(1734–1783) lieutenant in the palace guard who became Catherine the Great's lover, ally, and father of her third child.

Peter III—(1728–1762) incompetent, brutal ruler of Russia and husband of Catherine the Great. Peter became Russia's ruler on January 5, 1762, and ruled for about six months until his death.

abdicated—formally gave up power.

serfs—workers who could not legally leave the estate of the master they worked for.

Peter the Great—Peter I (1672–1725), ruler of Russia from 1682 to 1725. Peter built St. Petersburg, helped bring crafts and industry to Russia, and opened Russia to influence from Western Europe.

smallpox—highly contagious, infectious disease caused by the smallpox virus. Smallpox created sores on the skin, shedding of dead skin, and scar formation. Death was often the result.

inoculation—method of introducing a weak, disease-causing virus into the body to protect the body from a more serious case of that or a similar disease.

(Tested vocabulary words used in the online vocabulary quiz are underlined.)

During Reading

Students can use the **Study Guide** on the next page to help them understand and enjoy the story and recognize its importance in history.

After Reading

Students can answer the **Questions to Consider** in the book as a way to deepen their interpretation of the selection.

1. Why was Catherine worried when she received the letter about Peter's death?

2. What is your opinion of Peter III? How would you describe him?

3. What examples of Enlightenment influence on Catherine can you find in this story?

4. In what ways was Catherine great?

Bibliography

Catherine the Great

Kathleen Krull. *Lives of Extraordinary Women: Rulers, Rebels (And What the Neighbors Thought)* (2000). The life of Catherine the Great includes the reactions of her countrymen.

Leslie McGuire. *Catherine the Great* (1986). Recounts the story of the eighteenth-century Empress of Russia, describing her life as wife, mother, and ruler.

Milton Meltzer. *Ten Queens: Portraits of Women of Power* (1998). Includes a biography of Catherine the Great.

Gail Meyer Rolka. *100 Women Who Shaped World History* (1999). Includes a biography of Catherine the Great.

Peter the Great

Miriam Greenblatt. *Peter the Great and Tsarist Russia* (2000). Explains the role of Peter the Great in taking Russia into the modern world, describes the everyday life of the people, and includes poems, plays, and letters written by Russians about themselves.

Kathleen McDermott. *Peter the Great* (1991). A biography of the czar of Russia in the late seventeenth and early eighteenth centuries.

Diane Stanley. *Peter the Great* (1999). A biography of the czar who began the transformation of Russia into a modern state in the late seventeenth and early eighteenth centuries.

Life in Russia

E. M. Almedingen. *The Crimson Oak* (1983). Peter, a Russian peasant boy, 12 years old in the year 1739 and full of dreams, chances to cross paths with the exiled Princess Elizabeth and comes to realize his fate is linked to hers.

E. M. Almedingen. *Land of Muscovy: the History of Early Russia* (1972). Discusses the history and people of Russia during the fifteenth, sixteenth, and seventeenth centuries.

Name _____

Catherine the Great
by Carole Pope

1. How did Peter III react when Catherine seized his throne?

_____

_____

_____

2. What did Catherine do about the serfs that belonged to the Russian Orthodox Church?

_____

_____

_____

3. Why might people be afraid of the smallpox inoculation?

_____

_____

_____

4. Why did some people grumble about Catherine later in her reign?

_____

_____

_____

5. Essay Question
What do you think that Catherine might have done to help the serfs after she freed them?

Name _____

People and Terms to Know

This page lets you check your knowledge of the people and the terms used in "Catherine the Great." Find the best answer for each item. Then circle that answer.

1. Which person helped to open Russia to Western influence?

    a. Catherine II

    b. Grigory Orlov

    c. Peter III

    d. Frederick II

2. This was a serious disease that was contagious and often caused death.

    a. abdicated

    b. inoculation

    c. smallpox

    d. cancer

3. Which of the following terms means formally giving up power?

    a. abdicated

    b. inoculation

    c. smallpox

    d. serfs

4. This term describes a method of protecting the body from a serious disease.

    a. abdicated

    b. inoculation

    c. smallpox

    d. serfs

5. This Russian ruler improved Russia by building roads and opening up free trade.

    a. Catherine II

    b. Grigory Orlov

    c. Peter III

    d. Peter the Great

Answer Key

Catherine the Great
by Carole Pope

After Reading

1. Some observers thought Catherine was worried about the loss of her reputation. She may have worried about being thought of as a murderer or even accused of murder.

2. Answers will vary. Students should focus on Peter's cruel, foolish, and unpredictable behavior in their descriptions. Students might select from the many adjectives used in the story to describe Peter.

3. Students may say that she thought for herself, took over the Russian Orthodox Church to lessen its influence in government, and tried to free the poor people. She welcomed philosophers and journalists to show that Russia was not a backward country and brought new ideas about inoculation from London.

4. Answers will vary. Students may select any of Catherine's accomplishments mentioned in the story.

Study Guide

Answers will vary. Possible answers follow.

1. He panted, sobbed, ran around the palace, fainted, recovered, drank wine, and wrote two orders against her. He kept changing his mind and finally abdicated the throne. He wrote her sad notes that made the court laugh.

2. She took over the Church property, including the serfs, making them property of the government. Then she freed them.

3. Some students may say that people weren't very educated and didn't know a lot about science. It must have seemed frightening to have someone poke your skin with the very disease that you were trying to keep from getting.

4. People said that she helped the upper class but didn't help the serfs. She had freed them, but they still lived like slaves and were very poor. She also didn't allow the peasants to revolt when they weren't pleased with what she did.

5. **Essay Question** Some students may say that she could have seen that they got land to farm or trained them for other jobs. Accept any answer that reflects some thought about how one ruler can improve the life of a million poor peasants who had never done anything but work land for the nobles.

Building Vocabulary

Answers: 1. d, 2. c, 3. a, 4. b, 5. a.

Thomas Jefferson

BY LYNNETTE BRENT

Before Reading

Background

The story "Thomas Jefferson" shifts from Europe to America during the time of the American Revolution. Thomas Jefferson was born in the Blue Ridge Mountains of Virginia. His father was a self-educated surveyor who had acquired a sizeable estate and 60 slaves. Thomas's mother raised two sons and six daughters, but it is believed that Thomas's relationship with her was not very good. From the time of his father's death when Thomas was fourteen, he boarded with the local schoolmaster to learn Latin and Greek. In 1760, at the age of sixteen, he entered William and Mary College in Williamsburg.

Thomas was shy and very serious. He was said to be an obsessive student in college. He would spend 15 hours in study and three practicing his violin. This left only 6 hours for eating and sleeping. Thomas was primarily influenced by William Small, a Scottish-born teacher of mathematics and science, and George Wythe, the leading legal scholar in Virginia. After practicing law with Wythe for five years, he left Williamsburg to represent small planters in cases involving land claims.

Jefferson was torn between two loves. He was an extremely private person, but he felt called to public service. He entered the Virginia legislature just as opposition to the taxation policies of the British Parliament was heating up. At the same time, he built his own private haven at Monticello.

When Jefferson married Martha Wayles Skelton, her dowry more than doubled his land holdings and slaves. Two years later he wrote a paper summarizing his views on the rights of people in British America. It was published without his permission and moved him into the forefront as an advocate of American independence. He stated that the American colonies were tied to Great Britain only by people's voluntary bonds to the king.

In the spring of 1775, Jefferson was appointed by the Virginia legislature as a delegate to the Second Continental Congress. It is somewhat ironic that the man who would write arguably the most famous document on human equality in world history arrived in Philadelphia accompanied by three slaves.

John Adams asked Jefferson to prepare the first draft of a document explaining why a break with Great Britain was justified. The part of the document that begins "We hold these truths to be self-evident . . ." is still considered to be the foundation on which American political culture is based. With its reference to the equality of men, the rights of life, liberty, and the pursuit of happiness, and the institution of governments through the consent of the governed, Jefferson encapsulated the thought of major Enlightenment thinkers such as Locke and Rousseau.

Although he had been elected governor of Virginia in 1779, an embarrassing loss to the British, coupled with the death of his beloved wife in 1782, made Jefferson vow that he would never again desert his family for his country. Fortunately for the United States, that vow was broken when Jefferson became the third president of the new nation in 1801.

Preteaching the Story

As background, direct students to pages 20–21, "American Revolution." Use the story title as a starting point for students. Ask students what they know about Thomas Jefferson. What do they think he might have had to do with the Enlightenment? What do they expect to learn from the story? Record students' predictions and expectations.

Fact or Fiction?

The narrator is a fictional composite of Jefferson's school companions. All other people mentioned are historical figures; events are historically accurate. Dialogue is taken from recorded episodes in Jefferson's life.

Students will find sources for this story at the back of their book, on page 183.

Tie-in to History and Geography

The American Revolution in which Thomas Jefferson played so large a part can be traced in part to the long-standing rivalry between England and France to become the leading power in Europe. As the British settlers established colonies along the Atlantic coast of North America, the French developed their own settlements to the north and west. They called this New France. When British settlers began moving west across the Appalachians, conflict with the French was almost assured. The British colonists counted on British military support. Native Americans were recruited on both sides.

The French and Indian War (1754–1763) established the British as the dominant power in North America. Their world prestige had reached a new height, but so had the debt they had built up in fighting the French on three continents. Because they had helped the colonists, the British felt justified in taxing them to help pay their debt. Resistance against the various taxes levied by the British Parliament over the next decade, along with the laws that increasingly controlled the colonists' lives and economy, eventually brought the colonies together. They began to think of themselves as one people, rather than as 13 separate colonies.

The ideas of the Enlightenment were not confined to Europe. Educated men began to rethink the purpose of government and to assert their rights. The American Revolution and the beginning of an independent United States of America were the result.

People and Terms to Know

Thomas Jefferson—(1743–1826) author of the Declaration of Independence and third president of the United States, serving from 1801 to 1809. One of America's greatest thinkers, Jefferson was also a farmer, author, statesman, diplomat, scientist, and architect.

Williamsburg—capital of the English colony of Virginia in North America. It was a fine place to learn politics and observe government. Among its grand buildings were the College of William and Mary and the Governor's mansion. Sessions of the colonial legislature met in Williamsburg, as did the General Court.

Francis Fauquier (FAW•keer)—(c. 1704–1768) English administrator of the colony of Virginia who took an interest in the young Thomas Jefferson.

George Whythe (wihth)—(1726–1806) American lawyer and statesman who was a signer of the Declaration of Independence. He was a mentor to the young Thomas Jefferson.

House of Burgesses—legislature of the Virginia Colony. It was the first representative assembly in the American colonies (1619).

(Tested vocabulary words used in the online vocabulary quiz are underlined.)

During Reading

Students can use the **Study Guide** on the next page to help them understand and enjoy the story and recognize its importance in history.

After Reading

Students can answer the **Questions to Consider** in the book as a way to deepen their interpretation of the selection.

1. What did you learn about Thomas Jefferson from reading this story that you did not know before?

2. How did Thomas Jefferson's early years prepare him to become a great leader of the American Revolution?

3. How did Dr. Small influence Thomas Jefferson?

Bibliography

Thomas Jefferson

Shannon Lanier and Jane Feldman. *Jefferson's Children: The Story of One American Family* (2000). Follows the lives of Jefferson's children. Includes his association with slave Sally Hemmings.

James Meisner, Jr. and Amy Ruth. *American Revolutionaries and Founders of the Nation* (1999). Discusses the lives of John Adams, John Jay, Thomas Jefferson, and others.

Robert M. Quackenbush. *Pass the Quill, I'll Write a Draft: A Story of Thomas Jefferson* (1989). Follows the life and accomplishments of the third president, from his birth in 1743 to his retirement to Monticello.

Michael V. Uschan. *America's Founders* (1999). Discusses the influence of five great Americans, including Thomas Jefferson.

The American Revolution

Christopher Collier and James Lincoln Collier. *The American Revolution, 1763–1783* (1998). Examines the people and events involved in the significant war in which the thirteen original colonies broke away from England.

Don Nardo. *The American Revolution* (1998). Offers opposing viewpoints on the American Revolution, including prewar disputes, patriot versus loyalist views, wartime concerns, and debate among modern historians.

Michael Weber. *The American Revolution* (2000). Traces the history of the American Revolution, from the Boston Massacre to the British surrender at Yorktown.

Life in Colonial America

Barbara Brenner. *If You Were There in 1776* (1994). Demonstrates how the concepts and principles expressed in the Declaration of Independence were drawn from the experiences of living in America in the late eighteenth century.

Milton Meltzer, ed. *The American Revolutionaries: History in Their Own Words, 1750–1800* (1993). Letters, diaries, memoirs, interviews, ballads, newspaper articles, and speeches depict life and events in the American colonies in the second half of the eighteenth century.

Sarah Wister, Suzanne L. Bunkers, Megan O'Hara, ed. *A Colonial Quaker Girl: The Diary of Sally Wister, 1777–1778* (2000). The diary of the sixteen-year-old daughter of a prominent Quaker family who moved to the safety of the countryside during the Revolutionary War.

Monticello

Robert Young. *A Personal Tour of Monticello* (1999). Presents a tour of Thomas Jefferson's home in Virginia through the eyes of a slave boy, a cook, a visitor, Jefferson himself, and his granddaughter.

Name

Thomas Jefferson
by Lynnette Brent

1. How did Tom's college days help him to play an important role in politics later in his life?

2. What risk did Tom have to watch out for in college?

3. How did living in Williamsburg help to expand Tom's knowledge?

4. How do we know from information in the story that Tom eventually got over his depression over Martha's death enough to once again serve his country?

5. Essay Question
What ideas from the Enlightenment might have contributed to what Thomas Jefferson wrote in the Declaration of Independence?

Name _____

People and Terms to Know

This page lets you check your knowledge of the people and the terms used in "Thomas Jefferson." Find the best answer for each item. Then circle that answer.

1. This person was a Virginia lawyer who acted as a mentor for Thomas Jefferson.

   a. Thomas Jefferson

   b. Francis Fauquier

   c. George Whythe

   d. William Small

2. This term refers to the first representative body of lawmakers in Virginia.

   a. College of William and Mary

   b. House of Burgesses

   c. Congress

   d. Williamsburg

3. Which of the following people was a governor of the colony of Virginia before the Revolution?

   a. Thomas Jefferson

   b. Francis Fauquier

   c. George Whythe

   d. William Small

4. This was the capital of the English colony of Virginia.

   a. Monticello

   b. House of Burgesses

   c. Richmond

   d. Williamsburg

5. Which of the following people wrote the Declaration of Independence?

   a. Thomas Jefferson

   b. Francis Fauquier

   c. George Whythe

   d. William Small

Answer Key

Thomas Jefferson
by Lynnette Brent

After Reading

1. Answers will vary. Some students may say his early years prepared him to become a leader because his father made sure he had a good education.
2. He received a good education. His time in Williamsburg broadened his experience of life and exposed him to new ideas. His practice of law and service in the legislature helped prepare him for a leading role in government.
3. Dr. Small introduced Tom to the ideas of the Enlightenment thinkers and helped Tom to understand how important learning was. He introduced Tom to Governor Fauquier and to George Whythe, who also helped him in his learning.

Study Guide

Answers will vary. Possible answers follow.
1. He studied several different foreign languages and was a student of philosophy, science, music, and ethics. He could have used much of this knowledge later in serving as a representative and writing the Declaration of Independence.
2. Tom realized that he enjoyed a good time and risked being drawn into bad company. He was distracted by parties, dancing, and horse races. As he became aware of these dangers, he learned to keep away from them and enjoy respectable people.
3. Williamsburg gave Tom access to information from all over the colonies through the local newspaper. He was also able to meet and listen to the ideas of many statesmen as they debated the rights of the colonists and called for rebellion.
4. Martha died in 1782. According to the description of Thomas Jefferson in the text, he was president of the United States from 1801 to 1809. Therefore, he must have reentered the political world after Martha's death.

5. Essay Question Students familiar with the opening words of the Declaration of Independence should recognize the ideas of Enlightenment thinkers such as Locke and Rousseau. These ideas included equality, the rights of life, liberty, and the pursuit of happiness, and the idea that governments are formed only through the will of the people who agree to be governed. Students may also mention the ideas in the Primary Source feature. Accept any answer that relates to both Jefferson's ideas and the ideas of the Enlightenment.

Building Vocabulary

Answers: **1.** c, **2.** b, **3.** b, **4.** d, **5.** a.

"Let Them Eat Cake"

BY WALTER HAZEN

Before Reading

Background

The success of the American Revolution led many people in Europe to rethink the way their rulers treated them. In "Let Them Eat Cake," we see what happened in France at the end of the 1700s.

The wars of Louis XIV had left France with a huge debt. In 1715, Louis XV began his reign and France enjoyed several decades of peace. However, the debt remained, and Louis XV spent even more on building projects largely benefiting the upper class. When taxes did not produce the needed revenue, Louis borrowed from bankers. Some say that he didn't care what happened later, as long as he got what he wanted during his own reign. By the time he died in 1774, the moral and political authority of the crown had declined.

Louis XVI succeeded to the throne at the age of 19. He was immature and lacked self-confidence. Although he was generally a kind man, he had been raised to be king and had little knowledge of the common people that he ruled. He lacked the strength of character to control his court. The aristocrats opposed fiscal, economic, and administrative reforms that might have appeased the people, and Louis gave in to their demands.

When Louis called the Estates-General in 1789, there was already great unrest. The government's financial crisis had worsened and the harvest of 1788 had been poor, making food very expensive. Although the meeting gave people hope, they did not know whether the Estates-General could solve their problems because it hadn't met for 175 years. In addition, it was known that the people themselves, the third estate, had little chance of outvoting the other two estates—the Church and the nobles. One clergyman who would go on to become a leading revolutionary expressed the grievances of the people in these words: "What then is the Third Estate? Everything; but an everything shackled and oppressed. What would it be without the privileged order? Everything; but an everything free and flourishing. Nothing can succeed without it; everything would be infinitely better without the others."

Louis XVI's queen, Marie Antoinette, added fuel to the people's fire. The daughter of the Holy Roman rulers Francis I and Maria Theresa, Marie married Louis when she was 15. By the time Louis ascended to the throne, Marie had overcome her boredom with him by surrounding herself with frivolous friends. She was an easy target because of her behavior and alleged extramarital affairs and, to a large extent, because she was Austrian.

After the storming of the Bastille, Marie successfully prodded Louis to resist the attempts of the National Assembly to abolish feudalism and limit royal authority. Popular agitators attributed the famous "let them eat cake" to her, but it may have been a characterization of the way they felt she *would* have responded, rather than anything she actually said.

The overthrow of the monarchy was probably due more to the people's hatred of Marie Antoinette than any strong feelings they may have had for Louis.

Preteaching the Story

To give students background for the story, have them read pages 22–23, "French Revolution." Use the story title as a starting point for students. Ask if anyone is familiar with the quotation. Who do they think said it? What do they expect the story to be about?

Pronounce words from the story that may give students trouble such as guillotine (GEE•uh•teen), Antoinette (an•twah•NET) and Versailles (vuhr•SY).

Fact or Fiction?

Armand is fictional. Louis XVI and Marie Antoinette are historical figures and the events in the story are part of historical record. Students will find sources for this story at the back of their book, on page 183.

Tie-in to History and Geography

The reasons for the French Revolution are many, but there are five that are commonly mentioned. First, France had the largest population in Europe, but could not feed it adequately. Second, the middle class, or bourgeoisie, had expanded, but despite their wealth, they had been excluded from political power as in no other European country. Third, the peasants recognized the problems and did not support the traditional but oppressive feudal system. Fourth, the *Philosphes* of the Enlightenment, who advocated social and political reform, were more widely read in France than anywhere else. The increasing numbers of bourgeoisie familiar with these ideas put tremendous pressure on the monarchy. Finally, French participation in support of the colonies during the American Revolution had completely ruined an already weakened economy.

People and Terms to Know

feudal system—social and economic system in which serfs or peasants worked the land for nobles, who in turn provided armies for the rulers.

guillotine (GEE•uh•teen)—machine that uses a heavy falling blade to execute people by chopping off their heads.

monarchy—form of government headed by a king, queen, emperor, or similar ruler.

Louis XVI—(1754–1793) king of France from 1774 to 1792. Louis was king when the French Revolution began in 1789.

Marie Antoinette—(1755–1793) Austrian princess who married France's King Louis XVI in 1770. She was the daughter of the Hapsburg ruler Maria Theresa, the empress of Austria, and queen of Hungary.

middle class—class between the very wealthy and workers without special skills. Merchants and businessmen are part of the middle class.

French Revolution—political upheaval that began in France in 1789. This revolution overthrew the monarchy and brought democratic changes to France.

Versailles (vuhr•SY)—very grand royal palace just southwest of Paris.

Estates-General—French national assembly from 1302 to 1789. It was made up of representatives from the three estates, or classes: the clergy (church officials), the nobility, and the common people. It approved laws the king made, but did not make laws itself.

limited monarch—ruler whose powers are restricted by law.

absolute monarchies—governments by kings or similar rulers who have unlimited power.

(Tested vocabulary words used in the online vocabulary quiz are <u>underlined</u>.)

During Reading

Use the **Study Guide** on the next page to help you understand and enjoy the story and recognize its importance in history.

After Reading

Answer the **Questions to Consider** in the book as a way to deepen your interpretation of the selection.

1. What conditions in France led to revolution in 1789?

2. What was the Tennis Court Oath?

3. What event caused the revolution to take a more violent turn?

4. Based on what happened in the French Revolution, what advice would you have given Louis XVI and Marie Antoinette?

Bibliography

The French Revolution

Charles Dickens (adapted by Linda Jennings). *A Tale of Two Cities* (reissue 1996). This classic novel begins in the years leading up to the French Revolution and reaches its climax in the Reign of Terror.

Adrian Gilbert. *The French Revolution* (1995). Begins with the 1793 death ride of Louis XVI, moves backward in time to the causes of the bloody revolution, and outlines the years of horrific murders and treachery—in less than 50 pages. Includes the faults of the old regime—unjust taxation, reform failures, and widespread food shortages. The establishment of the National Assembly and its resultant massive killings are discussed.

Margaret Mulvihill. *The French Revolution: Bastille and Guillotine* (1989). Describes the causes, events, and aftermath of the French Revolution in 1789.

Steven Otfinoski. *Triumph and Terror: The French Revolution* (2000). Discusses the causes, events, and aftermath of the revolution that began in 1789 with the overthrow of the monarchy and ended ten years later with the rise of the Napoleonic dictatorship.

Gail B. Stewart. *Life During the French Revolution* (1995). This book covers both the political events and the social history during the period of the French Revolution.

Helen Maria Williams. Ed. by Jane Shuter. *Helen Williams and the French Revolution* (1996). Letters written by an Englishwoman who lived in Paris during the Reign of Terror. They provide a vivid account of life during this violent period.

Rachel Wright. *Paris, 1789: A Guide to Paris on the Eve of the Revolution* (1999). Uses a travel guide format to show what life was like in Paris at the time of the French Revolution.

Marie Antoinette

Kathryn Lasky. *Marie Antoinette: Princess of Versailles Austria-France, 1769* (2000). In 1769, thirteen-year-old Maria Antonia Josepha Johanna, daughter of Empress Maria Theresa, begins a journal chronicling her life at the Austrian court and her preparations for her future role as queen of France. Includes information about the history of the period, a family tree, and contemporary portraits.

Fiona MacDonald. *The World in the Time of Marie Antoinette* (2000). Recounts the story of Marie Antoinette and looks at what was happening all around the world in her time.

Name _____

"Let Them Eat Cake"
by Walter Hazen

1. What happened when the feudal system ended in France?

_____

_____

_____

2. What were some of the foolish actions of Marie Antoinette that made the people dislike her?

_____

_____

_____

3. Why might Marie have said something like "Let them eat cake" when she was told that the people had no bread?

_____

_____

_____

4. Why did the French people storm the Bastille?

_____

_____

_____

5. Essay Question
   What role do you think the Enlightenment played in the French Revolution?

Name _____

People and Terms to Know

This page lets you check your knowledge of the people and the terms used in "Let Them Eat Cake." Find the best answer for each item. Then circle that answer.

1. This term describes a group of people that included merchants and businessmen.

   a. limited monarch

   b. middle class

   c. French Revolution

   d. Estates-General

2. Which of these is the best description of Marie Antoinette?

   a. woman who was a leader in the French Revolution

   b. French noblewoman in the court of Louis XVI

   c. member of the French middle class

   d. Austrian princess married to a French king

3. Which term describes an assembly of representatives that approved laws the king made?

   a. limited monarch

   b. middle class

   c. French Revolution

   d. Estates-General

4. This term describes an uprising of the French people that began in 1789.

   a. limited monarch

   b. middle class

   c. French Revolution

   d. Estates-General

5. Which term describes a ruler whose powers are restricted by law?

   a. limited monarch

   b. middle class

   c. French Revolution

   d. Estates-General

Answer Key

"Let Them Eat Cake"
by Walter Hazen

After Reading

1. Students should mention a weak king, wasteful spending, the separation of social classes, privileges for the nobles, and poverty of the peasants. The growing middle class was also an important factor.

2. An oath taken by members of the Estates-General on a tennis court when they had been locked out of their meeting place. They vowed not to leave until they had given France a written constitution.

3. Louis gathered troops at his palace at Versailles in 1789. The people feared he would stop the work of the National Assembly.

4. Answers will vary. Students may suggest that they should have paid more attention to what the people wanted and needed and less on preserving their own power. Accept any reasonable answer.

Study Guide

Answers will vary. Possible answers follow.

1. Every person became equal under the law. The French gained freedom of speech and the press and won the right of assembly.

2. She made Louis build her a village of farmers' cottages at Versailles so that she could dress up and play peasant. She gambled on horses and threw fancy parties. She was spoiled and threw tantrums.

3. Some students might say that Marie was so unaware of what life was like outside the royal court that she really thought the people had a choice—if they didn't have bread, they could always eat cake or something else. Others may suggest that she didn't care about the people and that it was a sarcastic remark.

4. Louis XVI had gathered troops around him at Versailles. The people thought that he intended to stop the National Assembly so they took matters into their own hands and stormed the Bastille.

5. Essay Question Students should recall that Paris was the gathering place for many of the greatest thinkers of the Enlightenment, so the French would have been more familiar with their ideas than people in other countries. They would probably have done more thinking about individual freedom, rights, and what a government should and shouldn't do. Accept any answer that relates the actions of the revolutionaries to the ideas of the Enlightenment.

Building Vocabulary

Answers: **1.** b, **2.** d, **3.** d, **4.** c, **5.** a.

Text Pages 131–145

Toussaint L'Ouverture

BY BARBARA LITTMAN

Before Reading

Background

The story "Toussaint L'Ouverture" reminds the reader that the Americans and French were not the only ones who revolted during the 1700s.

When Christopher Columbus sighted the island he called Hispaniola in 1492, he thought he had reached India. He referred to the gentle Taino and Arawak peoples who lived there as Indians. Within 100 years, it no longer mattered what they were called because most of the indigenous people had disappeared—killed by warfare, disease, or being worked to death in the gold mines. The Spanish had thinly settled the eastern end of the island, but the western end was the home of French pirates. In 1697, the western third of the island was formally ceded to France by Spain. It was named Saint Domingue.

For nearly 100 years, Saint Domingue was the most important and wealthiest French overseas territory—the "Pearl of the Antilles." Half a million slaves were brought in to work its plantations where sugar, rum, coffee, and cotton were produced. Hatred and unrest grew with the cruelty of the French plantation owners.

Inspired by the success of the American and French Revolution, the slaves rebelled. A huge, imposing slave by the name of Dutty Boukman stood before his people and declared that "God who has created the shining sun above . . . is watching us and sees the misdeeds of the whites! The God of the whites demands crime. Our God is benevolent. Our God who is so good orders us to take vengeance!"

The slaves attending the meeting returned to their plantations. A week later, on August 24, 1791, a revolution that was anti-slavery, anti-colonial, and a call for social change for "the wretched of the earth" began. Boukman never saw the results of his call. He was beheaded in November 1791.

As the story tells, Francois Dominique Toussaint, later called Toussaint L'Ouverture, led the Haitian independence movement. He was an energetic man who was known as a healer, but as a fervent Catholic, he was opposed to voodoo. When the revolt began in 1791, Touissant was as yet uncommitted. After helping his former master escape, he joined the rebels and soon realized how inept their leaders were. Touissant collected his own army and trained them in guerilla tactics. His success is described in the story.

Touissant stopped fighting the French when they freed all of the slaves, but he eventually drove the slave-holding Spanish from the island and dictated a constitution that made him governor general for life with near absolute powers.

Still, he refused to declare the island independent from France. As he grew older and weary, Touissant continued to venerate France, yet knew that Napoleon hated blacks and would return slavery in order to restore the island to profitability. After Touissant was taken by the French, other black leaders who also feared a return to slavery led a successful campaign against the French army, which had been decimated by yellow fever. On January 1, 1804, the entire island was declared independent under its original Arawak name, Haiti.

Preteaching the Story

As background, have students read page 23, "Revolution in Haiti." Pronounce Toussaint L'Ouverture (too•SAN loo•vehr•TYOOR). Have students study the picture on page 132. What do they expect the story to be about? What do they think they may learn from reading this story? Record students' predictions and expectations.

Help students to pronounce other names that may give them problems, such as Leclerc (luh•KLER) and Maximilien Robespierre (MAK•suh•MIHL•yuhn ROHBZ•peer).

Fact or Fiction?

The characters and events in the story are real. There is some speculation about who Boukman really was and whether the meeting that sparked the revolution included a voodoo ceremony.

Students will find sources for this story at the back of their book, on page 183.

Tie-in to History and Geography

Explain that Columbus was not the first person to reach the Americas, but that for a long time, it was said that "Columbus discovered America." He actually landed on several islands in what are now known as the West Indies.

The island that Columbus named La Isla Espanola (Hispaniola) is actually divided into Haiti and the Dominican Republic. Have students locate a map of the West Indies and identify the island of Hispaniola. Explain that the revolt began in the northwestern part of the island and eventually spread throughout both the French and Spanish sections of the island. Some students may enjoy finding out more about the turbulent history of the island since the slave revolt.

People and Terms to Know

Touissant L'Ouverture (too•SAN loo•vehr•TYOOR)—(1743–1803) Haitian slave who became the leader of Haiti's successful attempt to gain independence from colonial rule.

Haiti—today, a republic in the West Indies on the island of Hispaniola. (The Dominican Republic is also on this island. The West Indies is a long chain of islands between Florida and South America.) Haiti was controlled by the Spanish from the 1500s until 1697. Then it was controlled by the French. Toussaint L'Ouverture led a slave revolt that eventually gained Haiti its independence in 1804.

Charles Leclerc (luh•KLER)—(1772–1802) French general and brother-in-law of Napoleon, whom Napoleon appointed to lead the French invasion of Haiti after Toussaint and his followers beat the English and Spanish.

"Declaration of the Rights of Man"—charter of rights and liberties adopted by the French national Assembly in 1789.

Maximilien Robespierre (MAK•suh•MIHL•yuhn ROHBZ•peer)—(1758–1794) extremist leader of the French Revolution who eventually was executed.

Boukman—(died 1791) Jamaican-born slave and priest of an African religion who was an important leader of the Haitian slave revolt. Self-educated, Boukman always carried a book, and got the nickname "Bookman."

Napoleon—(1769–1821) famous French general and conqueror who was emperor of France from 1799 until 1814, when he was exiled. He regained power for a short time during 1815, and then was exiled again.

(Tested vocabulary words used in the online vocabulary quiz are underlined.)

During Reading

Students can use the **Study Guide** on the next page to help them understand and enjoy the story and recognize its importance in history.

After Reading

Students can answer the **Questions to Consider** in the book as a way to deepen their interpretation of the selection.

1. What were the reasons that each of the three groups in Haiti—black slaves, whites, and mulattos—was unhappy?

2. How did the French and American revolutions influence events in Haiti in the 1790s?

3. How did Toussaint and his rebels beat their enemies?

4. Why did Sonthonax free the Haitian slaves?

5. Why do you think Toussaint L'Ouverture is important in world history?

Bibliography

Touissant L'Ouverture

Ann Griffiths. *Black Patriot and Martyr: Toussaint of Haiti* (1970). Biography of the eighteenth-century Haitian who led the revolution against French domination in the Caribbean.

Thomas and Dorothy Hoobler. *Toussaint L'Ouverture* (1990). A biography of the eighteenth-century slave who led his people in the struggle for an independent Haiti and became its ruler in 1799.

Walter Dean Myers. *Toussaint L'Ouverture : The Fight for Haiti's Freedom* (1996). A collection of paintings by Jacob Lawrence chronicling the liberation of Haiti in 1804 under the leadership of General Toussaint L'Ouverture.

Discovery of the Americas

George DeLucenay Leon. *Explorers of the Americas Before Columbus* (1989). Examines the voyages of explorers who reached the shores of North America before Columbus. Discusses Eric the Red, Leif Ericsson, the Norse settlements, and ancient visitors to South and Latin America.

Steve Low. *The Log of Christopher Columbus: The First Voyage: Spring, Summer, and Fall 1492* (1992). A simple adaptation of excerpts in Columbus's diary, from his departure from Spain to his landing in the New World in 1492.

Napoleon

Harry Henderson. *The Age of Napoleon* (1999). Discusses French history under the influence of Napoleon Bonaparte's rise from lowly origins to military and political power, his fall from power, and the legacy he left to Europe.

Haiti and the West Indies

Martin Hintz. *Haiti* (1998). Describes the geography, history, government, people, and culture of the second oldest republic in the Western Hemisphere.

Alison Hodge. *The West Indies* (1998). Presents an overview of the geography, climate, economy, government, people, and culture of the West Indies including the Dominican Republic and Haiti.

Mary C. Turck, Eric Black. *Haiti: Land of Inequality* (1999). Examines the history of Haiti's ethnic conflict and its effect on the people of that country.

Slave Revolts

Patricia C. and Fredrick L. McKissack. *Rebels Against Slavery: American Slave Revolts* (1998). A description of the slave revolts in the United States that were inspired by the example of Toussaint L'Ouverture.

Name

Touissant L'Ouverture
by Barbara Littman

I. What story did Father Baptiste tell Touissant that inspired him?

2. Why were Spain, England, and France so anxious to own a part of Haiti?

3. What was Boukman's plan for revolt?

4. How was Touissant deceived by the French?

5. Essay Question
Do you think that the slaves could have gotten their freedom in any way except a violent revolt?

Name _____

People and Terms to Know

This page lets you check your knowledge of the people and the terms used in "Touissant L'Ouverture." Find the best answer for each item. Then circle that answer.

1. Who was a slave from Jamaica and an important leader of the Haitian slave revolt?

   a. Touissant L'Ouverture

   b. Leclerc

   c. Boukman

   d. Napoleon

2. This is a republic in the West Indies.

   a. France

   b. Haiti

   c. Boukman

   d. Napoleon

3. This man was emperor of France.

   a. Touissant L'Ouverture

   b. Leclerc

   c. Boukman

   d. Napoleon

4. This man led Haitians to independence.

   a. Touissant L'Ouverture

   b. Leclerc

   c. Boukman

   d. Napoleon

5. What is the best description of the Declaration of the Rights of Man?

   a. part of the Declaration of Independence

   b. preamble to the United States Constitution

   c. charter of rights and liberties adopted by the French National Assembly

   d. charter adopted by the Haitians after the revolution

Answer Key

Touissant L'Ouverture
by Barbara Littman

After Reading

1. The slaves were unhappy because of the cruel treatment they received and because they weren't free. The white plantation owners couldn't sell their goods to any country but France. The mulattos had wealth and freedom, but did not have full citizenship.
2. The success of the French and American revolutions made the Haitians feel that they could also succeed in a revolt against the government.
3. They forced them to fight on ground that they weren't accustomed to. They would use guerilla tactics where they had women and children move through the trees to make it seem as if there were a lot of them and when they frightened the French soldiers, a few Haitians were able to defeat them.
4. The French had to fight against both the English and the Spanish. The only way that he could get enough people to fight on the French side was to free the slaves and hope that they would want to become free French citizens and fight for France.
5. Answers will vary. Students may suggest that he led one of the few successful slave revolts in history and that he paved the way for Haiti to become independent.

Study Guide

Answers will vary. Possible answers follow.
1. He told him the story of Spartacus, the slave who led a successful slave revolt in the Roman Empire.
2. It was the wealthiest European colony in the Americas and provided almost half of Europe's coffee, sugar, and cotton, making a lot of money for the colonizing country.
3. At the same time of night, all over the island, thousands of slaves revolted, setting fire to the plantations and cities.
4. Leclerc asked Touissant to meet him to discuss a settlement. He agreed to guarantee Touissant's freedom, but he lied and took him prisoner.

5. **Essay Question** Some students may realize that the slaves had no legal means to change the way the plantation owners treated them. They were treated like property, and the only way they could make the whites free them was to revolt. Other students may say that they could have tried to form groups of representatives to reason with the plantation owners, or they could have tried simply not working to make their point.

Building Vocabulary
Answers: **1.** c, **2.** b, **3.** d, **4.** a, **5.** c.

Tomatoes Are Poison and Potatoes Cause Leprosy

BY DEE MASTERS

Before Reading

Background

"Tomatoes Are Poison and Potatoes Cause Leprosy" tells the story of the Columbian Exchange. It covers a period from the Spanish conquest of the Aztecs to recent exchanges between the continents.

In the years after the first contact of Columbus in the West Indies, major interaction between the New World and the Old World began. As countries such as Spain and Portugal discovered the riches of this new land, they sent explorers and military expeditions to conquer more of the Americas. Colonists brought with them the trappings of their lives in the Old World. The interchange between the Americas and the Old World changed the lives of people on both continents.

The European diet changed as foods from the Americas arrived. These included potatoes, corn, tomatoes, and beans. Horses and cattle, brought to the New World by the Spaniards, changed the lives of Native Americans. Although they provided new means of transportation and labor, as well as new food sources, these large animals weren't a totally positive gift because they adapted quickly, destroying vegetation and competing with the native populations for food.

Goats, sheep, chickens, and even house cats traveled across the Atlantic with the Europeans, while North America gave Europe the turkey, squirrel, and muskrat.

Along with the positive exchanges, there were many negative consequences of the Columbian Exchange. Rats traveling on the ships spread diseases and wiped out many small native animals. Measles, typhus, plague, and smallpox devastated the indigenous peoples of the Americas, who had no immunity to them. It is estimated that between 50 and 90 percent of native populations died. This also changed the ethnic makeup of much of Latin America.

Sugar was another long-term producer of change. At one time, sugar was considered a luxury item. As sugar cane spread to the Americas, the Caribbean became the world's center of cane sugar. Because there was a worldwide demand, slaves were imported to work the plantations. Land was cleared for more acreage—the first large-scale assault on the rain forests.

We are still experiencing the effects of the Columbian Exchange. In addition to the examples given in the story, non-native weeds threaten to force out native grasses. Kudzu, brought for forage from Japan, has taken over in the southeastern United States. Insects such as Japanese beetles, Africanized (killer) bees, and the Gypsy moth threaten crops and people. And as the story suggests, exchanges now take place in hours, not months.

Preteaching the Story

To provide background for the story, have students read page 25, "The Columbian Exchange." Use the story title as a starting point. Ask students who might make a statement like that. Have students study the picture and read the caption. What do they expect the story to be about? What do they think they may learn from reading this story? Record students' predictions and expectations.

Help students with the pronunciation of difficult words in the story, such as Tenochtitlán (tay•NOCH•teet•LAHN), and Montezuma (mahn•tih•ZOO•muh).

Fact or Fiction?

The people in the story are historical figures and the events are historically accurate. Students will find sources for this story at the back of their book, on page 184.

Tie-in to History and Geography

In addition to the Columbian Exchange, another kind of trade was taking place from about 1518 to the mid-1800s. It was called triangular trade. In the first leg of the trip, merchants shipped cotton goods, weapons, and liquor to Africa. These were traded for slaves or gold. The second leg, called the Middle Passage, involved the shipment of the slaves across the Atlantic to the Americas. The traders sold the slaves for goods produced on the plantations.

In the final leg, these goods traveled to Europe where they were traded for manufactured goods that could be sold in the Americas. Some of the plantation products were also sent to Africa for more slaves.

The Middle Passage is the most infamous leg of this triangle of trade. Millions of African men, women, and children made the 21-90 day voyage. The ships were loaded with from 150 to 600 persons and slaves were often chained in the holds to keep them from rebelling or jumping overboard. There was little food and water and no sanitation. Deaths during the Middle Passage have been estimated at 13 percent, but may have been up to one-third of the "passengers." So many bodies were thrown overboard that sharks regularly followed the ships.

Show students a map of the trade routes during the Columbian Exchange and triangular trade. Have students figure out what cargoes might have been carried in each direction.

People and Terms to Know

Hernán Cortés (ER•nahn kahr•TEHZ)—(1485–1547) Spanish conqueror of Mexico. When Cortés arrived in Mexico, he established a city called Vera Cruz and burned his ships to prevent his soldiers from trying to go home.

Tenochtitlàn (tay•NOCH•teet•LAHN)—Aztec capital under Montezuma, center of an advanced civilization. It covered more than five square miles with 140,000 people, and had an elaborate guild system and a thriving economy.

Montezuma (mahn•tih•ZOO•muh)—Montezuma II (1456–1520), Aztec emperor of Mexico. Montezuma controlled a vast and wealthy empire that included today's Honduras and Nicaragua. His palace covered 10 acres and had 300 rooms.

epidemic—rapid spread of an illness, usually affecting many people.

Columbian Exchange—transfer of plants, animals, and diseases between the Western Hemisphere and the Eastern Hemisphere that began with Columbus's first voyage.

manioc (MAN•ee•ahk)—root crop that came from South America. It grows well in damp, hot areas.

leprosy—disease of the skin, flesh, and nerves which results in sores, scaly scabs, paralysis, and gangrene.

AIDS—disease caused by strains of a virus called HIV (human immunodeficiency virus) that attacks certain white blood cells. This deadly disease is spread through exchange of body fluids.

(Tested vocabulary words used in the online vocabulary quiz are underlined.)

During Reading

Students can use the **Study Guide** on the next page to help them understand and enjoy the story and recognize its importance in history.

After Reading

Students can answer the **Questions to Consider** in the book as a way to deepen their interpretation of the selection.

1. Why did smallpox cause so much damage to the Native American population?

2. What in your own words is the meaning of the "Columbian Exchange"?

3. What Old World import started the plantation system?

4. What was good and bad about the potato becoming the main food of Europe's poor people?

5. What lessons from the Columbian Exchange could we apply to the future?

Bibliography

Columbian Exchange

Gene Brown. *Discovery and Settlement: Europe Meets the New World, 1490–1700* (1995). Presents primary source materials related to the discovery and settlement of America and daily life in the colonies, including the experiences of Native Americans, African Americans, and women.

Laura Fischetto. *All Pigs on Deck: Christopher Columbus' Second Marvelous Voyage* (1991). Relates the events of Columbus's second voyage, focusing on the arrival of pigs in the New World.

Milton Meltzer. *The Amazing Potato: a Story in Which the Incas, Conquistadors, Marie Antoinette, Thomas Jefferson, Wars, Famines, Immigrants, and French Fries All Play a Part* (1992). Introduces the history, effects, and current uses of the potato in the world marketplace.

Penina Keen Spinka. *White Hare's Horses* (1991). In sixteenth-century California, a young Chumash Indian, White Hare, must find the courage to save her people from Aztec invaders with their frightening horses.

Aztecs

Robert Hull. *The Aztecs* (1998). Recounts the story of the Aztecs' rise to power and describes various aspects of their civilization including religion, arts and crafts, daily life, and legacy.

Nina Morgan. *Technology in the Time of the Aztecs* (1998). Examines the many aspects of culture in the Aztec society, including their food, clothes, buildings, industry, transport, warfare, and technology.

Scott O'Dell. *The Feathered Serpent* (1981). A young Spanish seminarian who the Mayas believe is their powerful god, Kukulcân, witnesses the coming of Cortés and the capture of the magnificent Aztec city, Tenochtitlan. (Fiction.)

Montezuma and Cortes

Deborah Crisfield, Patrick O'Brien. *The Travels of Hernán Cortes* (2000). A biography of the explorer whose brutal conquest of the Aztecs in Mexico was responsible for the first Spanish settlements in the New World.

Nathaniel Harris. *Montezuma and the Aztecs* (1986). Traces the life of the emperor who ruled the Aztec empire in Central America from 1503 to 1520 and discusses the history and culture of the Aztec civilization.

Sally Schofer Matthews. *The Sad Night: The Story of an Aztec Victory and a Spanish Loss* (1994). Tells how the Aztecs established an empire in Mexico and what happened when they, led by Montezuma, encountered Cortés and the Spaniards in the early sixteenth century.

Name _____

Tomatoes Are Poison and Potatoes Cause Leprosy
by Dee Masters

1. What were some of the reasons that Cortés was welcomed by Montezuma?

_____

_____

_____

2. What really conquered the Aztecs? How?

_____

_____

_____

3. What made 1492 an important date?

_____

_____

_____

4. Why did the Europeans begin to bring slaves to the Americas?

_____

_____

_____

5. Essay Question
   What, in your opinion, was the most important effect of the Columbian Exchange?

Name _____

People and Terms to Know

This page lets you check your knowledge of the people and the terms used in "Tomatoes Are Poison and Potatoes Cause Leprosy." Find the best answer for each item. Then circle that answer.

1. Who was the leader of an advanced culture in Mexico?

   a. Hernán Cortés

   b. Tenochtitlán

   c. Montezuma

   d. Columbian Exchange

2. Which term describes the trade between the Old and New Worlds?

   a. colonialism

   b. Tenochtitlán

   c. Montezuma's Revenge

   d. Columbian Exchange

3. Which is the best description of an epidemic?

   a. root crop from South America

   b. disease that attacks the skin and nerves

   c. rapid spread of a disease

   d. vast and wealthy empire

4. Who was a Spanish explorer who conquered the Aztecs?

   a. Hernán Cortés

   b. Tenochtitlán

   c. Montezuma

   d. Columbian Exchange

5. What was the capital city of the Aztecs?

   a. Mexico City

   b. Tenochtitlán

   c. Montezuma

   d. Columbia

Answer Key

Tomatoes Are Poison and Potatoes Cause Leprosy
by Dee Masters

After Reading

1. Smallpox didn't exist in the Americas before the Spaniards brought it, so the native peoples had never built up any immunity to it.

2. Answers will vary. Students should describe one or more aspects of the trade between the Old World and the New World.

3. Sugar cane.

4. Potatoes were cheap and easy to grow so even the poorest people could afford them. However, when the potato crop failed because of a plant disease, people died of starvation.

5. Answers will vary. Students may suggest that people should recognize that when a product is transported from one place to another, it will disturb the balance in the new area. Some students may say that we're already aware of possible problems. The rocks that were brought back from the moon were quarantined until it was certain they didn't carry a disease.

Study Guide

Answers will vary. Possible answers follow.

1. His men had horses that the Aztecs had never seen before. Natives who hated the Aztecs joined him against them. They believed that Cortés was Quetzalcoatl, an Aztec god.

2. Smallpox. It came from a black soldier in the Spanish army who infected the household in which he was housed. Because the Indians lived in such close quarters, the disease spread quickly. They had no immunity to it. After 60 days, there weren't enough Indians left to fight off the Spanish.

3. After that date, the Old World and New World remained in constant contact with one another as trade developed.

4. The plantations were very large and needed many workers. The Europeans didn't enjoy working in the tropical areas, so they brought in the slaves.

5. **Essay Question** Some students may suggest that it started the practice of slavery in the Americas. Others may say that the diseases that wiped out much of the indigenous population were the most important. Other students may select one of the crops or the animals. Whatever choice the students make, they should support their selection with reasons.

Building Vocabulary

Answers: **1.** c, **2.** d, **3.** c, **4.** a, **5.** b.

"And Yet, It Does Move!"

BY JUDITH LLOYD YERO

Before Reading

Background

Governments and the people they governed were not the only realms of new thinking during the years of the Enlightenment. Science was changing rapidly, from a domain shrouded in superstition and magic to an experimental approach to understanding nature, both personal and cosmological. "And Yet, It Does Move!" is the story of Galileo Galilei, one of the greatest names of the Scientific Revolution.

Since the days of the ancient Greeks, the explanations of nature proposed by Aristotle had been widely accepted. The Church had linked many of Aristotle's explanations with words from the Bible. Therefore, questioning Aristotle was seen as questioning the word of God. St. Thomas Aquinas even used one of Aristotle's arguments (that every motion had a cause) to prove the existence of God.

The traditional acceptance of ancient thinking received a major blow with the discovery of the New World at the end of the 1400s. Ptolemy had insisted that only the continents of Europe, Africa, and Asia could exist. He knew that the world was not flat and reasoned that if there were any other continents, people would have to walk upside down. (Obviously, an understanding of gravity wasn't very well developed.) With the discovery of the Americas, his theory was shown to be incorrect.

The Renaissance had shown human beings capable of creating great works of art, architecture, and literature. Why couldn't they delve into the mysteries of nature with equal skill?

The work of Copernicus, published after his death, stood the scientific and religious communities on their ear. Copernicus had observed and interpreted the movement of the planets. He used those observations to insist that the sun, not the earth, was the center of the cosmos.

Copernicus's work inspired others to study the heavens. Tycho Brahe, Johannes Kepler, and Galileo Galilei took different approaches to that study. It was Galileo's observations with the telescope that proved another of Aristotle's ideas incorrect. Heavenly bodies were not perfect spheres traveling in perfect circles around the earth.

All of this new thinking about science seriously threatened the authority of the Church, which was accustomed to dispensing and defending "truth." If people began arriving at "truths" themselves, where would that leave the Church? When people asserted their personal right to think for themselves, it was as revolutionary as their realization that they could decide how they wished to be governed.

Because of the times in which he lived and his own penchant for bluntness and lack of tact, Galileo was the most obvious target for the Church's wrath.

Preteaching the Story

Direct students to read the Background pages 24–25, "Scientific Revolution." Use the story title as a starting point for students. To what do they think the quote refers? What do they expect the story to be about? What do they think they may learn from reading this story? Record students' predictions and expectations.

Tell students that the story is about a scientist of the 1600s named Galileo Galilei (GAL•uh•LEE•oh GAL•uh•LAY) and a disagreement about whether the earth or the sun was at the center of the cosmos. Aristotle (AHR•ih•STAHT•l) and Nicolas Copernicus (koh•PUR•nuh•kuhs) were two other people involved in this issue.

Fact or Fiction?

The dinner party and guests in the opening scene are fictional, but they are based on social events of the times. Galileo Galilei and the events leading up to his imprisonment and trial are a matter of historical record.

Scholars agree that it is unlikely that Galileo uttered the words "And yet, it does move," as he left the trial. Although he undoubtedly believed them, he would have been foolish to take the chance that he might be overheard after what he had just experienced.

Students will find sources for this story at the back of their book, on page 184.

Tie-in to History and Geography

During the Middle Ages, heretics were seen as enemies of society. In 1231, Pope Gregory IX instituted the papal Inquisition to catch and try heretics. The word Inquisition comes from the Latin word *inquiro* meaning to "inquire into."

In general, a person suspected of heresy was given time to confess and absolve himself. If he refused, he was brought before the inquisitor, interrogated, and tried. Torture was not ruled out as a method of interrogation. If the Inquisition found the person guilty, a number of punishments were possible, ranging from prayer and fasting to imprisonment. However, only the secular authorities could impose the death sentence.

During the Spanish Inquisition during the 1400s, torture and cruelty reached its peak. About 2,000 "heretics" were burned at the stake. By the time Galileo appeared before the Inquisition, the methods had moderated, but it was still a very demeaning experience, and had Galileo not recanted, he might well have been turned over to the secular authorities for the death penalty.

People and Terms to Know

Galileo Galilei (GAL•uh•LEE•oh GAL•uh•LAY)— (1564–1642) Italian scientist and astronomer who made important scientific discoveries about motion. Galileo's experimental method became the basis for the scientific study of nature.

Aristotle (AHR•ih•STAHT•l)—(384–322 B.C.) famous Greek philosopher who studied and wrote about physics, astronomy, meteorology, plants, and animals. He described the world as made of four elements: air, earth, fire, and water, and said that motion is part of the "nature" of matter.

scientific method—logical procedure for gathering information about the natural world. It begins with a hypothesis, a suggested explanation. Then experiments are designed and observations are collected to test the hypothesis.

geocentric theory—earth-centered model of the universe. This theory says that the earth stands still while all heavenly bodies revolve around it. Supporters argued that if the earth moved, clouds and birds wouldn't remain overhead, and a ball thrown into the air would fall behind the person throwing it.

spheres—three-dimensional round objects such as globes or balls.

Nicholas Copernicus (koh•PUR•nuh•kuhs)— (1473–1543) Polish astronomer. He claimed that the sun is at rest near the center of the universe, and that the earth travels around the sun once a year.

heliocentric theory—sun-centered model of the universe. Today we know that the sun also moves around the center of the galaxy as the planets revolve around the sun.

(Tested vocabulary words used in the online vocabulary quiz are underlined.)

During Reading

Students can use the **Study Guide** on the next page to help them understand and enjoy the story and recognize its importance in history.

After Reading

Students can answer the **Questions to Consider** in the book as a way to deepen their interpretation of the selection.

1. Why do you think Aristotle believed that heavier objects would fall faster than lighter objects?

2. Why would Galileo say that the Bible shouldn't be used as a test for science?

3. What arguments did Galileo use for studying and interpreting nature in his own way?

4. Why did the Church put Galileo on trial in the court of the Inquisition?

5. What ideas have scientists proposed in modern times that were as shocking as Galileo's statement that the earth moves?

Bibliography

Galileo Galilei

Leonard Everett Fisher. *Galileo* (1992). Examines the life and discoveries of the noted mathematician, physicist, and astronomer whose work changed the course of science.

Paul W. Hightower. *Galileo: Astronomer and Physicist* (1997). Profiles the life of Galileo Galilei, focusing on his defense of the Copernican theory and his struggles with the Catholic Church.

Deborah Hitzeroth and Sharon Heerboth. *The Importance of Galileo Galilei* (1992). A biography of mathematician, physicist, and astronomer Galileo, from his early years to his confrontations with the Church, his last years, and his legacy.

Douglas McTavish. *Galileo* (1991). Describes the life and theories of Galileo relating how his discoveries conflicted with the accepted beliefs of his time.

Peter Sis. *Starry Messenger: a Book Depicting the Life of a Famous Scientist, Mathematician, Astronomer, Philosopher, Physicist, Galileo Galilei* (1996). Describes the life and work of the courageous man who changed the way people saw the galaxy by offering objective evidence that the earth was not the fixed center of the universe.

Michael White. *Galileo Galilei: Inventor, Astronomer, and Rebel* (1999). Describes the life and work of the scientist who was persecuted by the Inquisition for his views of the universe.

The Scientific Revolution

William Bixby. *The Universe of Galileo and Newton* (1995). Describes the careers of Galileo and the English mathematician Sir Isaac Newton and the scientific revolution created by their discoveries.

Harry Henderson and Lisa Yount. *The Scientific Revolution* (1996). Describes scientific discoveries that took place between 1550 and 1900, examines the development of the scientific method, and discusses the impact of science on people's views of their world.

Aristotle and Science

Steve Parker. *Aristotle and Scientific Thought* (1995). This book not only chronicles Aristotle's major philosophies, but also gives readers a quick overview of his world and times and explains how his ideas set him apart from his contemporaries. The chapter on Aristotle as naturalist/biologist, an area sometimes neglected in works on his life, is also noteworthy.

Name _____

"And Yet, It Does Move!"
by Judith Lloyd Yero

1. How did the cardinal react to Galileo's demonstration with the orange and grape?

_____

_____

_____

2. How did the scientific method differ from the way people had studied science in earlier times?

_____

_____

_____

3. Why do you think that Aristotle and later people wanted to believe that the earth was the center of the universe?

_____

_____

_____

4. Why do you think that Galileo agreed to the Inquisition's demands?

_____

_____

_____

5. Essay Question

If you had lived in the time of Copernicus and Galileo, would you have believed them?

Name _____

People and Terms to Know

This page lets you check your knowledge of the people and the terms used in "And Yet, It Does Move!" Find the best answer for each item. Then circle that answer.

1. This Polish scientist argued for the heliocentric theory.

   a. Galileo Galilei

   b. Aristotle

   c. Nicholas Copernicus

   d. Tycho Brahe

2. Which term describes a way of studying nature by experiment and interpreting observations?

   a. heliocentric

   b. geocentric

   c. philosophical

   d. scientific method

3. Which of the following is the best description of the geocentric theory?

   a. The earth is the center of the universe.

   b. The sun is the center of the universe.

   c. Heavy and light objects fall at the same rate.

   d. Everything in the heavens is a perfect sphere.

4. This ancient Greek philosopher explained nature.

   a. Galileo Galilei

   b. Aristotle

   c. Nicholas Copernicus

   d. Plato

5. This Italian scientist laid the groundwork for modern scientific study.

   a. Galileo Galilei

   b. Aristotle

   c. Nicholas Copernicus

   d. Tycho Brahe

Answer Key

"And Yet, It Does Move!"
by Judith Lloyd Yero

After Reading
1. Students may give an example, such as a feather and a stone, which fall at different rates. Because of friction and air resistance, heavier objects often do appear to fall faster than lighter ones.
2. He said that the Bible was as open to interpretation as any other book and questioned the interpretation of the Bible by Church scholars.
3. He said that God had given people their senses, reason, and intelligence. Surely God wanted people to use those abilities to decide what was true.
4. They had warned him not to teach anything more about the heliocentric theory. Galileo wrote a book in which he presented both the heliocentric and geocentric theories, but made the geocentric theory sound stupid. The Inquisition charged Galileo with believing false doctrine.
5. Answers will vary. Although these are not very recent, the idea that man could fly, that he could travel to the moon and beyond, and that he could communicate instantly with someone halfway around the world once seemed as impossible as Copernicus's heliocentric theory. Students may also mention ideas such as cloning. Accept any reasonable answers.

Study Guide
Answers will vary. Possible answers follow.
1. He said that it was just a parlor trick of some kind and didn't prove anything.
2. Early science was done by philosophers, not scientists. They simply thought about what they observed but never actually tested anything.

3. The earth was the home of man. People thought that man was the most important creature in the universe, so it made sense that man's home should be at the center.
4. Some students may say that he was old and afraid that they might kill him if he didn't do what they wanted. Others might say that he just wanted to get them off his back.
5. **Essay Question** Some students may say that they probably would be like others of the time and question an idea so different from what most people believed. Others may say that they would have looked at the evidence and made their own decisions. Danger from the Inquisition or having people think they were crazy may be suggested in students' answers.

Building Vocabulary
Answers: 1. c, 2. d, 3. a, 4. b, 5. a.

Lady Mary's Advice

BY STEPHEN FEINSTEIN

Before Reading

Background

At the same time that the new scientific thinking was being applied to motion on earth and in the heavens, others were applying the scientific method to the study of the human body. Advances in medicine were as startling as advances in chemistry and physics. "Lady Mary's Advice" tells of how the idea of inoculation for smallpox began.

In the same year that Copernicus's ideas were published (1543), Andreas Vesalius published an equally important book on anatomy. In the same way that Copernicus broke with the tradition of Aristotle, Vesalius questioned the ideas of Galen, an ancient Greek physician. Galen's ideas of anatomy had been drawn from the dissections of animals rather than humans. Human dissection was forbidden by Roman religion. Vesalius dissected cadavers and emphasized the accurate description of every part of human anatomy. His detailed drawings led to other discoveries, such as William Harvey's description of heart action and blood circulation.

Smallpox had been described as early as 1122 B.C. in China, and the mummified head of Pharoah Ramses V, who died in about 1152 B.C., showed signs of the disease. The virus may have been a mutation of an animal virus and spread through droplets of liquid from the infected person. From ancient times, the Brahmins of India are said to have prevented smallpox by the same method described in the story. Other peoples used the same idea, albeit in more bizarre ways. In China, people stopped up their noses with the incrustations of smallpox.

Transfer of the virus to broken skin with a needle was introduced into England by Lady Mary Wortley Montagu, wife of the English ambassador. Lady Mary had her own son successfully vaccinated in 1717. The court and aristocracy loudly approved the process, and the royal family even had two of their children inoculated in 1723. Despite this, inoculation met with violent resistance from physicians and clergy. The method was nearly forgotten until 1746 when Bishop Isaac Maddox of Worcester once more proclaimed its value. Medical effort through the eighteenth century concentrated on reducing the risks and side-effects of the inoculation process.

Edward Jenner had been a student of John Hunter, one of the most prominent surgeons in London in the mid-1700s. Hunter's advice was "Why think, [i.e. speculate]—why not try the experiment?" Jenner developed a broad interest in biological phenomena, superior powers of observation, and a reliance on experimental investigation.

Jenner was concerned about the unpredictability of inoculation (or variolation, named for the Latin name of smallpox, "variola"). Even as an apprentice, he had seen the connection between cowpox, a relatively harmless disease, and immunity to smallpox. In his famous experiment in May of 1796, Jenner infected a small boy, James Phipps, with cowpox. The boy developed a slight fever and minor lesion. On July 1, he inoculated Phipps with smallpox. No disease developed and he published his findings, calling his process "vaccination." *Vacca* is Latin for cow. Despite the fact that Jenner's "one-person trial" and the chance he took with the life of that person would be unacceptable today, there is no doubt that Jenner's method of vaccination led to the final eradication of smallpox.

Preteaching the Story

Use the story title as a starting point for students. Have the students look at the picture and read the caption. Ask students what they know about vaccinations. Many students may be unfamiliar with the smallpox vaccination because they are no longer required to get it. What do students expect the story to be about? What do they think they may learn from reading this story? Record students' predictions and expectations.

Fact or Fiction?

Lady Anne, her children, Countess Sofia, and Dr. Hacker are fictional characters. Lady Mary Montagu and her friend Dr. Maitland are historical figures. The methods of treating smallpox and the response of medical personnel to the process are historically accurate.

Students will find sources for this story at the back of their book, on page 184.

Tie-in to History and Geography

In 1977, the World Health Organization declared smallpox extinct. Only two cases had been seen in several years. Both of them had been caused by viruses kept in a lab. Although children are no longer vaccinated for smallpox on a regular basis, the vaccine must be kept by law in at least four laboratories around the world as a precaution against a future outbreak.

In the 1800s, when Louis Pasteur proposed the "germ theory" of disease and successfully developed weakened toxins to protect against full-blown diseases, he called them "vaccines" in honor of Jenner. Few vaccines are given through inoculation any more. Injections directly into the body are now the most common practice of administering vaccines.

People and Terms to Know

abroad—in a foreign country.

Lady Mary Montagu—(1689–1762) English letter writer and poet.

inoculate—to infect a person or animal with killed or weakened germs or viruses. The infected individual will suffer a mild form of the disease, but the body gets the protection from further, full-strength attacks of the disease.

(Tested vocabulary words used in the online vocabulary quiz are underlined.)

During Reading

Use the **Study Guide** on the next page to help you understand and enjoy the story and recognize its importance in history.

After Reading

Answer the **Questions to Consider** in the book as a way to deepen your interpretation of the selection.

1. Why did Lady Anne live in fear in the spring of 1721?

2. How did the Turks protect themselves against smallpox?

3. What usually happened to a person after receiving a smallpox inoculation?

4. Why do you think that Lady Mary Montagu wished to spread the word about the smallpox inoculation to others?

5. How would you compare the views of Dr. Hacker and Dr. Maitland about the risks of the smallpox inoculation?

6. If you had lived in London in 1721, what would you have decided was best for your family regarding smallpox inoculation?

Bibliography

Edward Jenner

Israel E. Levine. *Conqueror of Smallpox: Dr. Edward Jenner* (1960). A biography of the British physician who discovered vaccination as a means of preventing smallpox.

Stephen Morris. *Edward Jenner* (1992). A biography of the British physician who discovered the smallpox vaccine.

Vaccines

Margaret O. Hyde and Elizabeth H. Forsyth, M.D. *Vaccinations: From Smallpox to Cancer* (2000). An overview of vaccinations, their development, and their current and future use. Included are some basic terms, controversies concerning their use, and possible negative effects.

Smallpox

Norma Jean Lutz. *Smallpox Strikes!: Cotton Mather's Bold Advent Experiment* (1998). When a smallpox epidemic strikes Boston in 1721, 11-year-old Rob becomes the sole caregiver of his stepfather and brother during the time of their illness.

Robert Snedden. *Fighting Infectious Diseases* (2000). Discusses such infectious diseases as rabies, smallpox, AIDS, influenza, and malaria and describes how they are transmitted and treated.

The History of Medicine

Barbara Behm. *The Story of Medicine* (1992). Examines the practice of medicine from ancient times to the present and describes its current status regarding technological advances and differing levels of expertise in different parts of the world.

Phil Gates. *The History News: Medicine* (1997). Presents in newspaper format the stories of breakthroughs in medicine in many different cultures and lands from the year 8000 B.C. to the 1990s.

Anna Mountfield. *Looking Back at Medicine* (1988). Surveys the history of medicine from its beginnings in ancient Egypt and Greece through the development of hospitals, various discoveries on treating diseases, and medicine in the future.

Name _____

Lady Mary's Advice
by Stephen Feinstein

1. How had Countess Sofia met Lady Mary?

_____

_____

_____

2. Why do you think that a medical practice that was common in Turkey took so long to catch on in England?

_____

_____

_____

3. What were the possible problems with inoculations against smallpox?

_____

_____

_____

4. How did Edward Jenner improve on the smallpox inoculation?

_____

_____

_____

5. Essay Question
   How do you think that people would have explained the spread of diseases before the discovery of germs or viruses?

People and Terms to Know

This page lets you check your knowledge of the people and the terms used in "Lady Mary's Advice." Find the best answer for each item. Then circle that answer.

1. This term refers to the rapid spread of a disease through a population.

   a. abroad

   b. inoculate

   c. smallpox

   d. epidemic

2. Which of the following is a disease that killed many people in England?

   a. abroad

   b. inoculate

   c. smallpox

   d. epidemic

3. This term is used to describe where people are when they are in a foreign country.

   a. abroad

   b. inoculate

   c. smallpox

   d. epidemic

4. Which is the best description of Lady Mary Montagu?

   a. English mother who was afraid that her children might get smallpox

   b. English woman who supported the use of inoculation to fight the spread of smallpox

   c. English countess who had traveled widely to Italy, Greece, and Turkey

   d. English doctor who refused to use the process of inoculation

5. Which of these terms refers to infecting a person with a mild form of a disease to protect them against a more severe attack?

   a. abroad

   b. inoculate

   c. smallpox

   d. epidemic

Answer Key

Lady Mary's Advice
by Stephen Feinstein

After Reading

1. She was afraid that her two young children would catch smallpox and die.

2. They scratched their skin and put on some of the liquid from the sores of a person with smallpox.

3. Most people got a mild form of the disease. When they were over it, they couldn't catch it again.

4. She had caught smallpox and been left with scars. She had her own child inoculated and he didn't catch smallpox. She wanted to help protect other children and adults during the outbreak in England.

5. Dr. Hacker had a closed mind and wouldn't even consider that inoculation might work. Dr. Maitland explained that there was the possibility that a person might get a serious case, but still recognized that it offered a good chance of protection.

6. Some students may say that they would be inoculated because the disease was so serious. They could die from it or be disfigured, so it wouldn't be worth the risk. Others might say that, because it hadn't been tested enough, they'd wait for a while to see whether something better came along. Students should support their choices with reasons.

Study Guide

Answers will vary. Possible answers follow.

1. They had met in Constantinople while both of them were abroad.

2. The English who had never traveled abroad might have seen the Turks as "less civilized" than they were and might not have trusted a medical process that came from there. Also, any news would not have traveled as quickly or been as widespread as is true today.

3. Sometimes people didn't get just a light case of the disease, but a more serious case. They could still die of it. Also, people could catch smallpox from a person who had been inoculated, so they risked spreading the disease.

4. He used material from cowpox sores instead of from smallpox sores. Cowpox wasn't as serious a disease in humans, so the risks weren't as great. It still kept people from getting smallpox.

5. Essay Question Some students might suggest that evil spirits passed from one person to another or that only certain people were being punished for doing something wrong. Other students might say that the smell of someone who was sick made other people sick. Accept any reasonable answer.

Building Vocabulary

Answers: **1.** d, **2.** c, **3.** a, **4.** b, **5.** b.